YOUR recipe could appear in our next cookbook!

Share your tried & true family favorites with us instantly at

www.gooseberrypatch.com

If you'd rather jot 'em down by hand, just mail this form to...

Gooseberry Patch • Cookbooks – Call for Recipes
PO Box 812 • Columbus, OH 43216-0812

If your recipe is selected for a book, you'll receive a FREE copy!

Please share only your original recipes or those that you have made your own over the years.

Recipe Name:

Number of Servings:

Any fond memories about this recipe? Special touches you like to add or handy shortcuts?

Ingredients (include specific measurements):

Instructions (continue on back if needed):

Special Code: **cookbookspage**

Over ➤

Extra space for recipe if needed:

Tell us about yourself...

Your complete contact information is needed so that we can send you your FREE cookbook, if your recipe is published. Phone numbers and email addresses are kept private and will only be used if we have questions about your recipe.

Name:
Address:
City: State: Zip:
Email:
Daytime Phone:

Thank you! Vickie & Jo Ann

Christmas
Comfort Foods

Filled to the brim with classic homestyle recipes
and sweet holiday memories for creating
a cozy holiday season.

Gooseberry Patch

An imprint of Globe Pequot
246 Goose Lane
Guilford, CT 06437

www.gooseberrypatch.com

1•800•854•6673

Do you have a tried & true recipe...

tip, craft or memory that you'd like to see featured in
a **Gooseberry Patch** cookbook? Visit our website at
www.gooseberrypatch.com and follow the
easy steps to submit your favorite family recipe.
Or send them to us at:

Gooseberry Patch
PO Box 812
Columbus, OH 43216-0812

Don't forget to include the number of servings your recipe makes,
plus your name, address, phone number and email address. If we
select your recipe, your name will appear right along with it...
and you'll receive a **FREE** copy of the book!

Contents

Dedication

To everyone who loves baking cookies with Grandma, shopping for just the perfect gifts, decorating the prettiest tree ever, and sharing the best comfort foods with family & friends.

Appreciation

To all of you who shared your most cherished recipes for a merry Christmas...thank you!

Warm
Holiday
Memories

Christmas
Comfort Foods

It's a Wonderful Life

Monica Britt
Fairdale, WV

I love hosting our family's annual Christmas party at our house. This year's theme was "It's a Wonderful Life." This has been my mom's favorite movie since I was a kid. To start off this festive occasion, I mailed George Bailey party invitations to the guests. Then, we put up a 12-foot live Christmas tree in the living room and flocked it, so that it looked snow-covered. Extra-large white lights adorned the tree. We added white feather boas for garland and an angel was placed on top! Gifts were wrapped in white paper, tied with forest-green ribbons. We framed and hung up a vintage movie poster and placed a bell on the coffee table for guests to ring. Everyone enjoyed helping angels get their wings! We set up several "grazing" stations with party food...one with a variety of options to customize your own sub, one with delicious potluck dishes and one with sweet desserts. Excitement grew as Emily and Hattie (my cousin and her daughter) arrived home from Hawaii for the holidays! We chatted, played games, decorated cookies, opened gifts and ate more than we should have. In the midst of all this commotion, I paused for a moment to look around at all the love, and realized that truly, it's a wonderful life!

Warm Holiday
Memories

Christmas Eve Memories

Sandy Coffey
Cincinnati, OH

Back in the 1950s, I was always a mischievous child. I could not contain my excitement about Christmas and Santa. One Christmas Eve, I just could not go to sleep. I must have drifted off, and then, like the Grinch, I awoke and crept into the living room to see all the toys and gifts. As I was trying to sneak one of the wrapped gifts back to my bedroom, a voice down the hall told me, "Get back in that bed!" Foiled in my attempt to see what Santa had brought me, I had to wait until morning light. I couldn't get my younger brother to wake up and help me. Finally, morning came and I was allowed to check out all the gifts. It makes for a fun "Gram the Great" story for all the kids in my family, big and small.

Aunt Jean Knows Santa!

Jean Johns Schmehl
Saint Marys, OH

I always told my nephews that I knew Santa personally and always reported to him, so he would know who had been naughty or nice. One year, my nephew Joe went along with my husband Dave and me to an open house at Christmas where Santa would be. It turned out that Santa was our neighbor. We walked in and Santa came right over and said, "Hi, Jean, how are you?" My nephew's eyes got as big as saucers and he exclaimed, "Aunt Jean, you really do know Santa." I sure made a believer out of him!

Christmas Comfort Foods

Mom & My First Cookbook

Janis Parr
Ontario, Canada

When I was six years old, I got a very special present at Christmastime. I could always be found in the kitchen with Mom, helping with stirring, measuring or setting the table. I had my own little apron I always wore, along with my own rolling pin, a tiny little egg beater, little tin pie plates, and plastic measuring cups and spoons. On this particular Christmas, there was a small box all wrapped up under the Christmas tree. It had my name on it! The box was too small to be the flannel pajamas that Mom made for me every Christmas. It was too big to be the bath powder I always looked forward to getting. When I opened that box, inside was a little cookbook made just for children. It was called, *Fun to Cook Book*. Inside were easy recipes that children would like to make, like Five-Minute Fudge, Yummy Strawberry Pie and Tropical Freeze. This neat little cookbook wasn't just fun recipes, though. The first chapter was called, "My First Day in the Kitchen" and it outlined all the various baking tools and their sizes and uses. The next chapter was called, "Safety First" and was followed by page after page of pictures and step-by-step instructions for all the child-friendly recipes that followed. Mom and I shared this cookbook and worked side by side, making the fun recipes designed just for children. The date on this little book is 1955, and I still have this treasured cookbook. Memories of Mom and me, this special little book and the time we spent together, warm my heart. The kitchen was my favorite place to be all those years ago, and still is to this very day.

Warm Holiday Memories

Warm & Cozy Pajamas

Kelli Wells
Coal City, IN

I remember when I was a child, we would celebrate Christmas Eve at my granny's house. All my aunts, uncles and cousins would be there. There were homemade cookies, candies and food everywhere. The most precious memory I have is of the Christmas when Granny made flannel pajamas for me and all my cousins. I changed into those warm and cozy pajamas as soon as I opened them up. Oh, what I'd give to go back to that time and feel the warmth of those jammies. My precious granny has since passed, but who knew all those years ago that one day, my own children would be so very blessed to have had flannel jammies made for them by her too. I have saved those warm and cozy flannel jammies. Maybe one day, my future grandbabies will be able to feel the warmth and love that Granny put into making them. What sweet memories.

Mom's Homemade Gifts

Carla Barnum
Las Vegas, NV

Mom made our Christmas the best she could by making special gifts for us. We didn't have a lot of money, so Mom made me enough clothes to wear a different outfit every day for a week! She also made clothes for my new Barbie and Ken dolls. I loved everything she made, but especially all the baked goods and candy. Mom kept her peanut butter fudge and other candy in boxes in the pantry. Of course, I had to "test" the candy, so when she was away, I went in the pantry to sample a few pieces. I rearranged the pieces, thinking she wouldn't notice. Years later, she admitted she knew all along! She was a good sport. Now her fudge is a family favorite that is requested every Christmas.

Christmas
Comfort Foods

A Very Special Santa Shop

Maryann Brett
Johnstown, PA

My mother lived in a nursing home for the last 16 months of her life. Those months became very special to both my mom and me as it allowed me to become "just her daughter" again, instead of being her caregiver. She truly loved her time there, and when she passed away on New Year's Eve in 2014, I knew she was happy. As a way to honor her and also as a way for me to give back for all the wonderful care she received, I decided to set up a "Santa Shop" with the help of a few church friends. What began as a one-time activity quickly grew for the next five years. While my mom lived there, I had realized that the residents had very few choices they made on their own. Someone else picked out their clothes, the meals were whatever the cook made for the day, the activities were planned by someone else. I decided to give them a day to choose what they wanted!

The activity room was filled with Christmas decorations of every kind. There were stockings for the residents' doors, Christmas books, handmade lap blankets and full-size fleece blankets, warm socks and hand lotions. But as simple as it sounds, the thing that touched me the most was watching the residents choose from an entire table of Christmas cards. Many people gave me Christmas cards for the table. To see each person pick the card they wanted that was addressed "To someone special," and to see their eyes light up as they opened that special card, brought me to tears on more than one occasion. Watching each resident get to choose anything they wanted in a room filled with all sorts of things was simply magical, and so heartwarming to every person who ever helped me on that day. I'm sure my mom beamed with pride from above as she watched her granddaughter Suzanne accompany me on those days. We also decorated a Christmas tree and "wrapped" every framed picture in the hallways to look like Christmas gifts. It was always a long day until we got it all done, and as we drove home each year in the dark, our hearts never felt fuller. We knew that we had been blessed to witness the joy that was shared by every person there, including the staff. That day each year, for the next five years after my mom passed away, was the true spirit of Christmas for me. It was a day that I always received way more than I ever gave.

Warm Holiday Memories

Christmas with My Memé

Teanda Smith
Saint Albans, ME

I don't know how many people still remember making homemade paper dolls, but it was something I did with my Memé all the time. She used to make us paper dolls along with little houses made of cardboard boxes. Our houses always had curtains and rag rugs. They even had beds made from plastic tomato containers. We would spend days working on them together. Nothing ever had to be done in a hurry...she truly loved spending time with me. As I got older, there weren't so many paper dolls, but we still spent time together. One year at Christmas when I was about twelve, instead of cutting small strips of paper for gift tags, we made paper dolls...big boys for the men, smaller ones for the boys and so forth. When I wrapped Memé's gift from me, her gift tag was a lady with a bun and glasses. She kept that tag forever hanging in her room. I had the greatest Memé ever. I miss her so much.

Christmas Comfort Foods

Drive-In Movies on Christmas Eve

Betty Kozlowski
Newnan, GA

Back in the late 1950s, Mom and Dad sent all but the youngest of us kids off to the drive-in theater on Christmas Eve so they could put the presents under the tree. The six of us were so excited to do this! It was the first time ever that we had gone anywhere without Mom or Dad. My oldest sister drove us, as the theater was not far from the house. When we pulled up, they attached the clunky old speaker to the driver's window. My older brothers and sisters conspiratorially planned that as soon as the movie ended, we would leave right away to avoid all the traffic to get home quickly. During the course of the movie, my brothers excitedly pointed to the sky and announced that they had seen Santa's sleigh, much to the delight of the younger ones. Once the movie ended, my sister quickly began to pull out into the lane to leave, only to be severely jerked back because, in her haste, she had forgotten to remove the speaker! What a laugh we had!

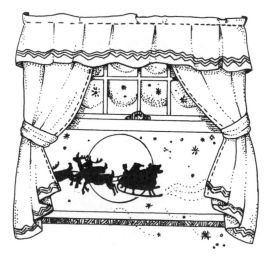

Warm Holiday Memories

Pizza for Christmas Eve

Brenda Montgomery
Lebanon, IN

Once my girls were older, we started a new tradition on Christmas Eve. They all come over and I make four pizzas, so that everyone has at least one favorite pizza and three others to try. When I'm starting to assemble the pizzas I ask for some help. My girls will come in the kitchen with me and we set up an assembly line. I get the crust spread out, then one does the sauce, then one does the meats and cheeses and puts them in the oven. Then we gather in the living room and get the presents passed out and open them. By that time the pizzas are done and we all get to sit around and talk about some of the fun we've had on Christmas Eves past.

S A N T A Tags

Blanche Neal
McKinney, TX

We all know the story of "Yes Virginia, there is a Santa Claus." Well, as my children and grandchildren began to question whether or not the jolly old man existed, I created special gift cards to put on their packages. The cards read: S-pecial A-nonymous N-iceness T-o A-nother-SANTA. It has become a tradition in our family. My children and grandchildren are now grown, with homes of their own now and continue the tradition. "Yes, there is a Santa."

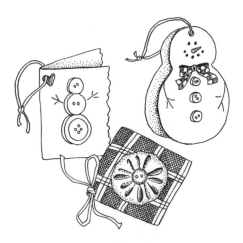

Christmas
Comfort Foods

Snowed In for Christmas

Karen Hallett
Nova Scotia, Canada

The Christmas I was eight, my sister, brother-in-law and their three children came the day before Christmas Eve to deliver gifts. By the way, I have a twin and the two of us were the youngest of 12 children. A few of my nieces and nephews are close to our age; three are older. Anyway, Christmas Eve started with light snow and it continued to get heavier. We soon discovered my sister's family was staying with us for Christmas. I was upset because Santa was not going to know the kids were at our house. I asked my mom if I could empty my bank and go to the store. My brother-in-law took me to the store, where I bought them each a very small toy and some chocolate. When we got back to the house, I wrapped the gifts and asked Mom to put them under the tree. My brother and I also asked Santa to give one of our gifts to the kids. Nearly 50 years later, my nephew mentioned this Christmas when we were talking one day. He said it was one of his greatest Christmas memories ever.

Warm Holiday Memories

Santa's Red Checkmark

Suzanne Matlosz
Mesa, AZ

When my youngest brother was little, Mom and Dad would wrap his gifts and place them under the tree. These were the "practical" gifts. All the toys mentioned in his letter to Santa were hidden in my bedroom closet. On Christmas Eve, after he went to sleep, I put on my elf cap and spent the evening wrapping all of his gifts. As for the gifts already under the tree, "Santa" would put a huge red checkmark on them, to let my brother know Santa had been there. He was so excited to see that red checkmark, because that meant Santa said he was a good boy and could open his gifts. I still think of those sleepless nights with happy memories.

Spreading Carols of Joy

Cindy Slawski
Medford Lakes, NJ

Each year through high school, my friends and I would go caroling in our neighborhood and then to the local nursing home to spread some Christmas cheer. We would often be invited into neighbors' homes for cookies or given small donations which would then be sent to our local food bank. After caroling, we always settled in at my house for popcorn, hot cocoa and a Christmas movie. Those moments are some of my most treasured and I think of them fondly every Christmas.

Christmas
Comfort Foods

Reindeer Games

Sheri Kohl
Wentzville, MO

When our three girls were little, my husband brought his family's Christmas Eve tradition to our home. He would play some Christmas music and in between songs, there came a "Ho, ho, ho, Merry Christmas!" along with the sound of reindeer hooves he had recorded. The girls would stop whatever they were doing, look up in wonder and run out the front door to see if Santa and his reindeer were on the roof. Outside the front door was a wrapped package of new Christmas pajamas and a small trinket for each of them, along with a note from Santa saying he would be back later when they were sleeping to bring their gifts. We were able to do this for many years before they caught on. I still remember the looks on their sweet faces when they heard Santa.

Gingerbread Houses

Mary Motte
Henderson, NV

Our very much-loved tradition, which began when my kids were young, is to decorate small, individual gingerbread houses for our Christmas Eve dinner centerpiece. We choose a night when we can be sure that those coming from out of town will be here. I generally make and assemble the houses ahead of time. Then everyone gets their own piping bag of icing and bowls of candy are set in the center of the table. My kids are now adults, but we still share this tradition together. Many years, we have had friends join us and take their little houses home. It's a tradition we all look forward to!

Warm Holiday
Memories

Snowflake Fun

Toni Leathers
Claremont, CA

Growing up in the Chicago suburbs, we got tons of snow. We spent our Christmas vacation days sledding, skating and playing for hours with all the neighbor kids. One of my favorite memories was standing on our ice skating pond while it snowed, watching the snowflakes land on my coat sleeve. I would try to see if it was true that no two snowflakes are alike. They melted as fast as they fell. I remember being so excited and telling my sisters and friends that each snowflake was perfect. Then we had a snowball fight...such fun memories!

Christmas Santa Surprise

Tracie Digirolamo
La Place, LA

My twin daughters arrived seven weeks early, and we all arrived home a week before Christmas. Doctor's orders were to stay away from crowds, as the flu was bad that year. As a surprise on Christmas Eve, my brother-in-law came fully dressed in a beautiful Santa suit to take pictures with my newborn girls. He held them ever so gently. I would never had this picture if he hadn't taken the time to come and surprise us. It was wonderful!

Christmas
Comfort Foods

Handmade Christmas Stockings

Glenda Reynolds
Millersport, OH

There have been many memorable Christmases over my lifetime, but one particular memory will always stand above all of the rest. It was 2010, and that November, my dearest husband had passed away quite unexpectedly. Our family was reeling from this loss, not only myself, but my adult daughter and son, and their families including my sweet grandchildren. We simply could not imagine the holiday season without Paw. My daughter Becky readied a plan, unbeknown to me until a couple of days before Christmas Eve. She told me that all eight of my grandchildren and their parents would be spending the night on Christmas Eve in my home, the cherished farmhouse where I had raised my two children. Every grandchild came with their own sleeping bag and Christmas pajamas. All were so excited to lay down their bags next to each other and be with their cousins on this special night! As I minded the youngest one, my four-month-old Sophie, my son and daughter and their spouses were busy at our large kitchen table, cutting new Christmas stockings out of felt for each child, as they slept upstairs. Each felt stocking was designed and sewed with cute embellishments and the children's names, and then hung all filled with goodies by our fireplace. Then all the gift packages for each child were brought in by these special Santas...needless to say, the living room was wall-to-wall gifts. What a splendid sight, and yes, it did take all night! By five in the morning, we had a stampede down the steps and some wide-eyed, astonished children. I have not seen the likes of it again to this day. That evening and day will be recreated in my memory as every Christmas Day draws near. My sweet family set aside their own comforts and home celebrations to be with me, and oh, what a comfort! Those same stockings still grace my fireplace this holiday, though five of my now ten grandchildren are grown. Each one comes back, every Christmas Day to claim the surprises still nestled within, and to remember a time when we celebrated one another, even in our great loss.

Warm Holiday Memories

The Macaroni Shoe

Tracy Burdyshaw
Perry, OH

Every December in the mid 1960s, I got to ride the 40 miles our teacher drove to our little one-room country school in South Dakota, back to town with her. My teacher would drop me off at my grandparents' house and I'd be so excited. Grandma always had a special craft ready for me to make for my mom for Christmas. As the fifth child out of six, I felt so special that this was something that Grandma did with just me! The best ever was one year when Grandma gave me a high-heeled pump and I glued all sorts of shapes of macaroni to it. We spray-painted it gold, then green styrofoam was placed inside and artificial poinsettias added the beautiful final touch. My brothers and sisters still laugh and tease me to this day about the "macaroni shoe" gift, but at six years old, I thought it was glorious, as did my mother, who proudly displayed it for years.

Christmas Comfort Foods

A Christmas Church Dinner

Virginia Taylor
Louisville, KY

Our church's Christmas Sunday School pageant and dinner were held
the first Saturday in December. The ladies were dressed in their best red
and green, wearing holly berry and crochet bell corsages, as they rushed
around the church basement with their casserole dishes. The gentlemen
made sure a bedsheet "curtain" on a clothesline was properly tied across
the pulpit. The church was illuminated with wax candles as the lights
were dimmed except for the stage. Little feet were tapping from one side
to another and nervous giggles were heard. The cold air from the back
of the church rushed down the aisle and late-arriving parishioners found
a seat as the pageant began. At the end, "O Beautiful Star of Bethlehem"
would be played with everyone singing, as we all went to the basement
for a delicious dinner. Even the littlest angel with her aluminum foil
wings would stand in line, holding her own plate. So many wonderful
memories in the making!

Christmas in Germany

Kristi Edney
Bowie, MD

When I was three or four years old, we lived over in Germany because
my dad was in the Army. At Thanksgiving and Christmas, my parents
would invite servicemen for a meal because they could not go home for
the holidays. I remember one Christmas, one of the men brought me a
huge baby doll! That doll was as tall as I was and had beautiful long
blonde hair just like mine! I carried that doll around with me all
Christmas day and continued to play with her everyday. It's still a
favorite memory of mine.

Warm Holiday
Memories

Handmade Trains & Houses

Denise Evans
Moosic, PA

Every Christmas, my family had the most beautiful train platforms set up. My great-grandfather was from Germany and spent many hours in his workshop. He would make the most beautiful houses for the train platform. He was ahead of his time as he recycled small household items, such as using toothpaste caps to create little flowerpots to set outside these wonderful little houses. Christmas was truly his favorite holiday. He made our Christmases special as we watched the trains chug their way through the busy town of well-lit houses and through the winding mountains. My great-grandfather was 93 when he passed on Christmas Day. It was bittersweet. He passed, but he passed on Christmas Day...his favorite holiday!

Christmas Lights

Charlotte Zito
Virginia Beach, VA

Each year at Christmastime, our whole family makes travel mugs of hot cocoa and we pile into the family car to see the beautiful Christmas lights at our local botanical garden. The light show stretches for several miles throughout the garden and we sip cocoa, eat popcorn and point out our favorite displays. After enjoying the professional lights, we take the long way home through our neighborhood to take in the neighbors' yard displays. It's always a magical evening!

Christmas
Comfort Foods

A Special Christmas Gift

Janis Parr
Ontario, Canada

One Christmas, I wanted to give my daughter a special gift for Christmas, something that I had made for her and that she'd treasure for years to come. She has two horses that she had rescued and restored to good health. I thought it over, and decided to make her a gift with some of the beautiful hair from her horses' manes. I made two braids from their hair and wove them through an old horseshoe I'd found. I finished it off by adding a sprig of spruce from the pasture they enjoyed. My daughter was so delighted with this special gift, and as I saw the surprise and joy on her face when she opened her present, I was delighted too.

A Special Gift on Christmas Morning

DeeDee McCullough
Rochester Hills, MI

I grew up in a large family of eight children. We didn't have much, but we had everything! One Christmas my younger brother, who was about seven years old, kept asking for a remote-control car. We weren't in the habit of asking for specific gifts, but I guess my parents realized how much he wanted that car. They gathered the rest of us children and asked us if they could spend a little extra for his car, as the rest of us would get a less expensive gift. We all agreed. When he opened that box on Christmas morning there wasn't a dry eye in the room. I have never seen a child so excited and thankful to receive a gift. I have no memory of what I got for Christmas that year and it didn't matter. It was the best Christmas ever!

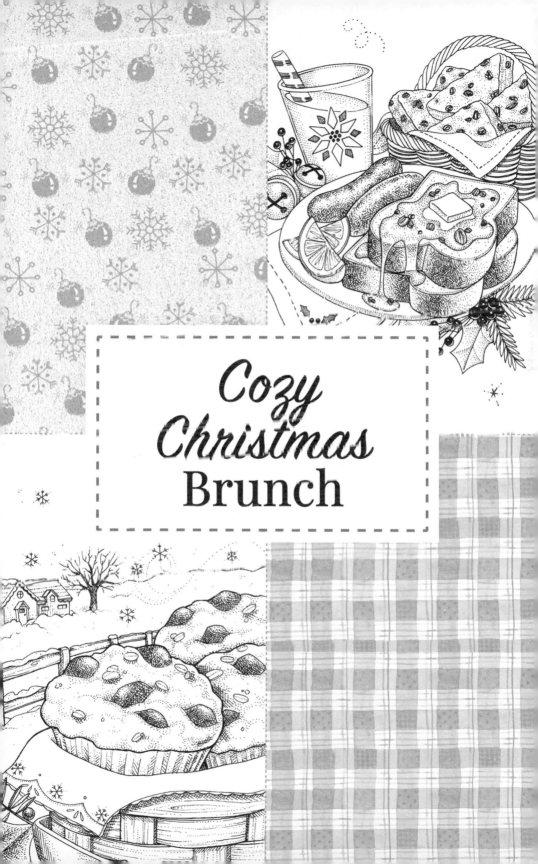

Cozy Christmas Brunch

Christmas Comfort Foods

Raspberry Cream Muffins

Linda Diepholz
Lakeville, MN

This is my favorite muffin recipe. It's so good, I used to take it to work to share with co-workers. Try it...I think you'll agree!

1 c. fresh raspberries
3/4 c. plus 2 T. sugar, divided
1/4 c. butter, softened
1 egg, beaten
1/2 t. almond extract
1/2 t. vanilla extract
2-1/4 c. all-purpose flour

1 T. baking powder
1/2 t. salt
1 c. half-and-half
1 c. white chocolate chips,
  finely chopped
2 T. brown sugar, packed

In a small bowl, toss raspberries with 1/4 cup sugar; set aside. In a large bowl, blend butter and 1/2 cup sugar. Beat in egg and extracts; set aside. In another bowl, combine flour, baking powder and salt; stir in butter mixture alternately with half-and-half. Fold in raspberry mixture and chocolate chips. Spoon batter into greased or paper-lined muffin cups, filling 3/4 full. Combine brown sugar and remaining sugar; sprinkle over batter. Bake at 375 degrees for 25 to 30 minutes, until a toothpick comes out clean. Cool muffins for 5 minutes in pan; remove to a wire rack. Serve warm or cooled. Makes one dozen.

Serve up freshly baked muffins any time! Place muffins in a freezer bag and freeze. To warm frozen muffins for serving, wrap in heavy foil and pop into a 300–degree oven for 12 to 15 minutes.

Cozy Christmas
Brunch

Egg & Bacon Breakfast Casserole

Nancy Jay
Minster, OH

This recipe was shared by my dear friend Ruth and has been our Christmas morning breakfast since 1987. I prepared the casserole before the kids woke up, put it in the oven when they came downstairs, then it was ready to serve when they were finished opening their gifts from Santa. To save time, the bacon can be cooked, crumbled and refrigerated the day before.

1/2 c. butter, sliced
6 c. unseasoned croutons
3 c. shredded sharp Cheddar
   cheese
1 doz. eggs

3 c. milk
3/4 t. dry mustard
1 lb. sliced bacon, crisply cooked
   and crumbled

In a 325-degree oven, melt butter in a 13"x9" baking pan for about 5 minutes. Remove pan from oven; tilt to coat entire pan. Scatter croutons over butter and sprinkle with cheese; set aside. Beat eggs in a large bowl; whisk in milk and mustard. Pour egg mixture over cheese and croutons; sprinkle with crumbled bacon. Bake, uncovered, at 325 degrees for 40 to 50 minutes. Let stand at room temperature for 5 to 10 minutes before serving. Makes 8 servings.

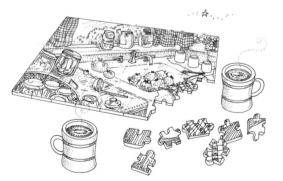

Enjoy a winter weekend retreat at home. Tuck dinner in
the slow cooker, then spend the day in your jammies.
Savor a leisurely brunch, do jigsaw puzzles, browse
holiday catalogs or re-read a favorite book.
What could be cozier?

Christmas Comfort Foods

Pineapple Upside-Down Pancakes

Tamara Long
Huntsville, AR

This is my go-to, ultimate, spoil-everyone breakfast treat.
Perfect for snow days and birthdays!

2 c. all-purpose flour
1/4 c. sugar
4 t. baking powder
1/2 t. salt
1 egg, beaten
1-1/2 c. milk
1/4 c. butter, melted and
　　slightly cooled
2 t. rum extract or vanilla extract

1 c. brown sugar, packed
20-oz. can pineapple rings,
　　drained
8 to 10 maraschino cherries,
　　drained
1/2 c. flaked coconut
Garnish: warm maple syrup
　　or whipped cream

In a bowl, mix together flour, sugar, baking powder and salt; set aside.
In another bowl, whisk together egg, milk, melted butter and extract.
Add flour mixture to egg mixture; mix well and set aside for 5 to
10 minutes. Spread brown sugar on a small plate; coat pineapple rings
with brown sugar on both sides. Add pineapple rings to a buttered
griddle or skillet over medium-high heat; cook until caramelized on both
sides. Add a cherry to the center of each ring; top with 1/4 cup pancake
batter and sprinkle with coconut. Cook until golden and bubbles pop
around the edges; flip and cook other side. Serve with warm maple
syrup or whipped cream. Makes 8 pancakes.

Try a new topping for pancakes and waffles. Agave syrup, honey,
fruit preserves and even caramel topping are all scrumptious, while a
sprinkle of chopped nuts or chocolate chips makes them extra special.

Cozy Christmas
Brunch

Cheesy Bacon Breakfast Muffins

Virginia Campbell
Clifton Forge, VA

These muffins are so good! The cooking aroma will wake up those sleepyheads. Make a double batch to keep in the fridge and reheat in the microwave for a quick meal or snack.

2 c. biscuit baking mix
2/3 c. buttermilk
1/4 c. canola oil
1 egg, beaten
1/8 t. red pepper flakes
1/2 c. sweet onion, chopped

1/2 c. green pepper, chopped
1 c. shredded sharp Cheddar cheese
8 slices sliced bacon, crisply cooked and crumbled

In a large bowl, combine biscuit mix, buttermilk, oil, egg and red pepper flakes. Stir just until moistened; fold in remaining ingredients. Spoon batter into greased muffin cups, filling 3/4 full. Bake at 375 degrees for 20 minutes, or until a toothpick inserted near the center comes out clean. Cool muffins in pan for 10 minutes; remove to a wire rack. Serve warm. Refrigerate any leftovers. Makes about one dozen.

Set the breakfast table the night before...enjoy a relaxed breakfast in the morning.

Christmas
Comfort Foods

English Muffin Loaves

Pat Martin
Riverside, CA

Get out the butter and jam for these satisfying slices of warm toast. The loaves travel well when we take them to family & friends on our trips and vacations. Bake, slice, toast and bring on the butter!

6 c. all-purpose flour, divided
2 envs. active dry yeast
1 T. sugar
2 t. salt

1/4 t. baking soda
2 c. milk
1/2 c. water
cornmeal for dusting

In a large bowl, combine 3 cups flour, yeast, sugar, salt and baking soda; set aside. In a saucepan, combine milk and water. Heat over medium-low heat until very warm, 120 to 130 degrees. Add to flour mixture; beat well. Stir in enough of remaining flour to make a stiff batter. Grease two, 8-1/2"x4-1/2" loaf pans; sprinkle each pan with cornmeal. Divide batter between pans; sprinkle tops of loaves with cornmeal. Cover and let rise in a warm place for 45 minutes. Uncover; bake at 400 degrees for 25 minutes. Immediately remove loaves from pans; cool on a wire rack. Slice and serve. Makes 2 loaves, 16 slices each.

A Christmas countdown! Get the family together and think up 25 fun activities like making gingerbread men, dancing to holiday music, sledding or reading a Christmas story. Write each on a December calendar, then do all the activities together.

Cozy Christmas Brunch

Holiday Pepper Jack Frittata

Edward Kielar
Whitehouse, OH

Red and green sweet peppers make this fast egg dish
perfect for holiday breakfasts.

1 red pepper, chopped
1 green pepper, chopped
3/4 c. shredded Pepper
   Jack cheese

15 leaves fresh flat-leaf
   parsley, chopped
7 eggs, beaten

Coat a 9" pie plate with butter-flavored non-stick vegetable spray.
Sprinkle peppers, cheese and parsley into pan; pour eggs over all.
Bake, uncovered, at 375 degrees for 30 minutes. Cool slightly; cut into
wedges. Makes 4 to 6 servings.

Easy Ham Quiche

Marie Lane
Fayette, MS

Growing up, our daughter was picky about breakfast food, but would
eat quiche. This is a great dish for breakfast, lunch or dinner.

9-inch pie crust, unbaked
2 5-oz. cans ham, chopped or
   broken up
1-1/2 c. shredded mozzarella
   cheese

2 eggs, beaten
4 t. mayonnaise

Arrange pie crust in a 9" pie plate; pierce crust all over with a fork.
Spread ham and cheese in crust; set aside. In a bowl, beat together
eggs and mayonnaise; pour egg mixture over all. Bake, uncovered, at
350 degrees for about 35 minutes, until crust is golden and center is
set. Let cool about 5 minutes; cut into wedges. Makes 6 servings.

Wake your family up to Christmas music...
such a nice way to begin the day!

Christmas Comfort Foods

Crab & Asparagus Quiche

Vickie
Gooseberry Patch

This scrumptious recipe makes its own crust. We think it's special enough for holiday guests at either brunch or lunch.

6 eggs, beaten
1/2 c. buttermilk baking mix
3/4 c. half-and-half
2 6-oz. cans crabmeat, well
    drained and flaked
1 c. asparagus, cut into 2-inch
    pieces and steamed

1 c. shredded Swiss cheese
1 T. dried, minced onions
1/2 t. salt
1/8 t. pepper

Whisk eggs in a large bowl; set aside. In another bowl, combine biscuit mix and half-and-half; add mixture to eggs and stir until smooth. Stir in crabmeat, asparagus, cheese and seasonings. Pour mixture into a buttered 9" deep-dish pie plate. Bake, uncovered, at 350 degrees for 45 to 50 minutes, until center is set. Cool in pan on a wire rack for 15 minutes; cut into wedges to serve. Serves 6.

Christmas Day is often too busy for families to get together for dinner. Instead, how about a family brunch the weekend before? Ask everyone to bring a breakfast casserole, a basket of muffins or another breakfast treat to share. You'll enjoy visiting, munching and exchanging gifts and have a much more relaxing holiday.

Cozy Christmas
Brunch

Brown Sugar Muffins

Lisa Barger
Conroe, TX

I've had this recipe so long, I don't remember where it came from!

1 c. light or dark brown sugar,
    packed
1/2 c. butter, melted
1 c. milk
1 egg, beaten

1-1/2 t. vanilla extract
2 c. all-purpose flour
1 t. baking soda
1/4 t. salt

In a large bowl, stir together brown sugar and butter. Add milk, egg and vanilla; stir until smooth. Add flour, baking soda and salt; mix just until moistened. Divide batter into 12 muffin cups sprayed with non-stick vegetable spray, filling 2/3 full. Bake at 375 degrees for 20 minutes, or until a toothpick inserted comes out clean. Makes one dozen.

Bacon-Cheddar Potato Cakes

Carolyn Deckard
Bedford, IN

My husband loves potato cakes and these are his favorite...
glad they are so easy to make! Hope you enjoy them
as much as we do.

3 slices bacon
4 c. cold leftover mashed
    potatoes
2 eggs, beaten

1 t. onion powder
1/2 t. salt
1/2 t. pepper
1 c. shredded Cheddar cheese

In a large deep skillet, cook bacon over medium-high heat, turning occasionally, until crisp and golden, about 10 minutes. Remove bacon to a paper towel, reserving drippings in skillet. In a bowl, mix together mashed potatoes, eggs and seasonings; stir in crumbled bacon and cheese. Form mixture into 8 patties. Heat reserved drippings over medium heat; add patties. Cook until crisp on both sides, about 4 minutes per side. Makes 4 servings.

Christmas Comfort Foods

Sausage & Bacon Bites

Melanie Lowe
Dover, DE

We can't stop eating these tasty treats! Perfect for brunch or appetizers, and a great make-ahead.

2 6.4-oz. pkgs. brown & serve
  breakfast sausages, cut
  in half

3/4 lb. sliced bacon, cut in half
1/2 c. plus 2 T. brown sugar,
  packed and divided

Wrap each piece of sausage in a piece of bacon. Place 1/2 cup brown sugar in a shallow bowl; roll sausages in sugar and secure with a wooden toothpick. Place in an aluminum foil-lined 15"x10" jelly-roll pan. Cover and refrigerate for 4 hours or overnight. Sprinkle wrapped sausages with one tablespoon brown sugar. Bake, uncovered, at 350 degrees for 35 to 40 minutes, turning once, until bacon is crisp. Sprinkle with remaining brown sugar. Makes about 3 dozen.

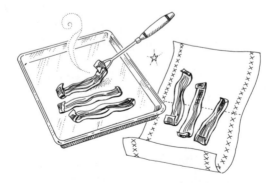

Here's a quick tip for bacon. Arrange slices on a baking sheet and bake at 350 degrees. It'll be crisp in about 15 minutes, with no messy splatters!

Cozy Christmas Brunch

Christmas Morning Bars

Elizabeth Smithson
Mayfield, KY

I have had this recipe for awhile. When my kids were home,
we always had a big breakfast on Christmas mornings. Everyone
loved these alongside warm sticky rolls. Memories, memories!

16-oz. pkg. ground pork
   breakfast sausage
2 8-oz. tubes refrigerated
   crescent rolls

2 c. shredded Cheddar or
   Swiss cheese
5 eggs, beaten
1/2 t. dried oregano

Brown sausage in a skillet over medium heat; drain well. Unroll one
tube rolls into an ungreased 13"x9" baking pan; press seams together.
Bake, uncovered, at 350 degrees for 5 minutes. Layer sausage, cheese,
eggs and oregano over baked crust. Unroll remaining tube of rolls; layer
on top. Bake, uncovered, at 350 degrees for 15 to 20 minutes. Cut into
squares. May be baked ahead and refrigerated; reheat in microwave.
Makes 12 to 15 servings.

Spicy Bacon Twists

Carol Lytle
Columbus, OH

These sweet & spicy bacon strips are irresistible!

1 c. light brown sugar, packed
1 T. dry mustard
1/2 t. cinnamon

1/2 t. nutmeg
1/4 t. cayenne pepper
1 lb. sliced bacon

Place a wire rack on an aluminum foil-lined rimmed baking sheet; set
aside. In a small bowl, stir together brown sugar and spices. Press each
slice of bacon into mixture until well coated. Twist each strip a few
times; place on rack. Bake at 350 degrees for about 30 minutes, until
bacon is browned and crisp enough to hold its shape. Serves 8.

It is Christmas in the heart that puts Christmas in the air.
– W.T. Ellis

Christmas
Comfort Foods

Golden Fruit Compote

Laura Fuller
Fort Wayne, IN

This is a recipe Mom tried one Christmas after finding it in a magazine. It was a hit! Wonderful at brunch, or with baked ham or pork. The canned figs aren't so easy to find anymore, but you can substitute dried figs simmered in water until they're plump.

29-oz. can peach halves, drained
29-oz. can pear halves, drained
20-oz. can pineapple rings,
   drained
15-oz. can Kadota figs, drained

1/2 c. brown sugar, packed
1/3 c. butter
1 t. ground ginger
3/4 t. curry powder
1/8 t. salt

Combine all fruits in a 2-1/2 quart casserole dish; set aside. In a small saucepan, combine remaining ingredients. Bring to a boil over medium heat; cook and stir until brown sugar dissolves. Drizzle mixture over fruit; mix gently. Bake, uncovered, at 350 degrees for 40 minutes, basting occasionally with liquid in dish. Serve warm. Makes 8 servings.

A sweet favor for children coming to your holiday brunch! Fill a basket with little bags of "Reindeer Food" for kids to sprinkle on the lawn on Christmas Eve. To make, simply mix cereal rings with candy sprinkles.

Cozy Christmas Brunch

Orange-Cranberry Walnut Muffins

Connie Litfin
Carrollton, TX

I make these muffins whenever I am having a group over to visit, or when I want to give some away. They are always a hit!

3 c. all-purpose flour
1-1/4 c. sugar
1 T. baking powder
2 eggs, beaten
1-1/4 c. milk

3/4 c. canola oil
2 T. orange oil (not extract)
1-1/2 c. chopped walnuts
3/4 c. dried cranberries

Combine flour, sugar and baking powder in a large bowl; set aside. In another bowl, combine eggs, milk and oils; mix well and add to flour mixture. Stir until moistened; fold in walnuts and cranberries. Spoon batter into 18 to 20 greased muffin tins, filling 2/3 full. Bake at 375 degrees for 18 to 20 minutes. Muffins freeze well. Makes about 1-1/2 dozen.

Gingerbread Coffee

Liz Blackstone
Racine, WI

Treat your guests to a coffee shop brew! The molasses mixture can be kept refrigerated and used as needed.

1/2 c. molasses
1/4 c. brown sugar, packed
1/2 t. baking soda
1 t. ground ginger
1 t. ground cloves

3/4 t. cinnamon
6 c. hot brewed coffee, divided
1 c. half-and-half
Garnish: sweetened whipped
   cream, cinnamon

In a small bowl, combine molasses, brown sugar, baking soda and spices; stir well. Cover and chill for at least 10 minutes. To serve, add 1/4 cup hot coffee to each of 6 coffee cups. Stir in one tablespoon of molasses mixture until dissolved. Fill cups with remaining hot coffee to within one inch of the top; stir in half-and-half to taste. Garnish with a dollop of whipped cream and a sprinkle of cinnamon. Serves 6.

Christmas
Comfort Foods

Overnight Egg Bake

Roxanne Anderson
Williams, IA

This is the egg bake my family insists on, every Christmas morning. For those who aren't big fans of vegetables, I make one pan with just ham and cheese. I'll also use browned breakfast sausage instead of ham. It is so easy to make the night before, and just pop it in the oven the next morning.

2 c. asparagus, cut into 1-inch
    pieces and steamed
1 green pepper, chopped
1 red pepper, chopped
1/2 onion, chopped
1 to 2 T. oil
8 slices white bread, crusts
    removed and divided
2 c. chopped ham, chopped
    and divided

3 c. shredded Cheddar cheese,
    divided
6 eggs, beaten
2 c. whole milk
10-3/4 oz. can cream of
    mushroom soup
salt and pepper to taste
2 c. corn flake cereal, crushed
6 T. butter, melted

In a saucepan over medium heat, sauté asparagus, peppers and onion in oil until slightly tender. In a greased 13"x9" glass baking pan, arrange 4 bread slices. Top with half each of vegetable mixture, ham and cheese. Arrange remaining bread slices on top; repeat layering. In a large bowl, whisk together eggs, milk, soup, salt and pepper until well combined; spoon over mixture in pan. Cover and refrigerate overnight. In the morning, combine corn flakes and melted butter; spread evenly over egg mixture. Bake, uncovered, at 350 degrees for one hour, or until center is set. Remove from oven; let stand about 10 minutes and cut into squares. Serves 10 to 12.

For a scrumptious honey-pecan bagel spread, blend 8 ounces softened cream cheese and 2 tablespoons honey. Fold in 1/2 cup toasted chopped pecans. Chill for one hour before serving...yum!

Cozy Christmas Brunch

Fluffy Bran Waffles

Karen Ensign
Providence, UT

*These tender waffles have become a staple for
Sunday morning breakfasts.*

2 eggs
2 T. sugar
1-3/4 c. milk
1/4 c. canola oil
2 t. vanilla extract

1-1/2 c. all-purpose flour
1/2 c. wheat bran
4 t. baking powder
1/2 t. salt
Garnish: butter, syrup or jam

In a large bowl, with an electric mixer on high speed, beat together
eggs and sugar for 3 minutes, or until fluffy. Beat in milk, oil and
vanilla; set aside. Add flour to a separate bowl; stir in wheat bran,
baking powder and salt. Add flour mixture to egg mixture. Beat on low
speed just until combined, but do not overmix; batter should have small
lumps. Spray a preheated Belgian waffle iron with non-stick vegetable
spray. Add enough batter to barely fill the grooves. Cover and cook
to desired crispness. Serve warm, garnished as desired. Makes about
8 to 12 waffles.

Chocolate Malted Milk Syrup

Robin Hill
Rochester, NY

*Scrumptious drizzled over waffles...yummy spooned over
cake and ice cream, too!*

1 c. whipping cream
1/2 c. malted milk powder

2/3 c. semi-sweet chocolate chips
1/2 t. vanilla extract

In a small saucepan over medium heat, warm cream until small bubbles
form around the edges. Reduce heat to low. Whisk in malted milk
powder; fold in chocolate chips. Cook, stirring often, until well blended
and chocolate chips have melted completely. Stir in vanilla. Serve warm.
Makes about 2 cups.

Christmas
Comfort Foods

Cheesy Scrambled Egg Bake

Lisa Gowen
Saint Charles, MO

*My neighbor shared this delicious recipe with me when I was
going to have a group over for breakfast. It was an
excellent choice...everyone loved it!*

4 T. butter, melted and divided
1/4 c. green onions, white part
   only, minced
4-oz. can diced green chiles
2 T. canned diced jalapeño
   pepper

16 eggs, beaten
1 c. whipping cream
1-1/2 t. kosher salt
1 t. pepper
1-1/2 c. favorite shredded cheese
1/2 c. green onions, thinly sliced

Coat a 13"x9" baking pan with 2 tablespoons melted butter; set aside.
To a non-stick skillet over medium heat, add remaining butter, minced
onions, chiles and jalapeño pepper. Cook until softened, about 5 minutes.
Remove from heat; cool to room temperature. In a large bowl, whisk
together eggs, cream, salt and pepper. Stir in cooled sautéed mixture,
cheese and sliced onions. Pour mixture into prepared pan. Bake,
uncovered, at 350 degrees for 10 minutes. Stir and bake another
10 to 20 minutes, until eggs are set to desired doneness. Transfer eggs
to a serving bowl and serve. Serves 8.

Old-fashioned favorites like a vintage
sled or a pair of ice skates by the front
door are a sweet welcome for friends.
Tie on evergreen boughs, pine cones
and red berry sprigs for cheery color.

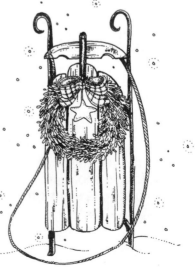

Cozy Christmas Brunch

Pam's Christmas Breakfast Pizza

Tammy Navarro
Littleton, CO

My twin sister Pam gave me this recipe over 25 years ago. I've served it on Christmas mornings annually ever since, with a fruit salad on the side and a pitcher of mimosas for the adults. It's truly become a tradition!

1 lb. ground pork breakfast
   sausage
2 8-oz. tubes refrigerated
   crescent rolls
1 c. frozen shredded
   hashbrowns, thawed

1 c. shredded Cheddar cheese
5 eggs, beaten
1/4 c. milk
1/2 t. salt
1/8 t. pepper

Brown sausage in a skillet over medium heat; crumble and drain. Meanwhile, arrange both tubes of crescent rolls side-by-side in an ungreased 13"x9" baking pan to form a crust, pinching seams to seal. Outer edge of crust should be slightly raised. Spoon sausage over crust; top with hashbrowns and cheese. In a bowl, whisk together eggs, milk, salt and pepper; spoon over crust. Bake, uncovered, at 375 degrees for 30 to 40 minutes, until eggs are set. Let stand 5 to 10 minutes; cut into squares. Serves 8.

Use favorite cookie cutters for all kinds of holiday fun. Trace around them onto colorful paper for placecards and package tags...add some glitter for sparkle. Cookie cutters can even serve as napkin rings or used to trim a wreath...clever!

Christmas Comfort Foods

Cranberry Coffee Cake

Agnes Ward
Ontario, Canada

This scrumptious cake makes a perfect hostess gift.

1/2 c. shortening
1 c. sugar
2 eggs
2 c. all-purpose flour
1 t. baking powder
1 t. baking soda

1 t. salt
1 c. light sour cream or low-fat
    plain yogurt
1 t. almond extract
1 c. whole-berry cranberry sauce
1/2 c. chopped pecans

In a large bowl, with an electric mixer on medium speed, beat together shortening and sugar. Beat in eggs, one at a time; set aside. In another bowl, sift together flour, baking powder, baking soda and salt. Add flour mixture to shortening mixture alternately with sour cream or yogurt and extract; beat well. Pour half of batter into a greased tube pan. Spoon cranberry sauce over batter in pan; cut through batter with a table knife to marble. Add remaining batter; sprinkle with pecans and press down lightly. Bake at 350 degrees for about 55 minutes, until a toothpick inserted near the center tests clean. Cool for 5 minutes; turn out of pan onto a serving plate. Drizzle Glaze over warm cake; slice to serve. Makes 16 servings.

Glaze:

1/2 c. powdered sugar
1 T. water

2 drops almond extract

Stir together all ingredients to a drizzling consistency.

Yes, Virginia, there is a Santa Claus. He exists as certainly
as love and generosity and devotion exist.

–Francis P. Church

Cozy Christmas Brunch

Chicken Divan Squares

Marsha Baker
Pioneer, OH

With a crescent roll crust, this is a little more dressed up than the classic divan. Roast turkey can be used instead of the chicken. Oh-so tasty!

2 c. broccoli, chopped
8-oz. tube refrigerated
   crescent rolls
1-1/2 c. cooked chicken, cubed
10-3/4 oz. can cream of
   chicken soup

1/2 c. mayonnaise
1/4 c. onion, finely chopped
2 t. Dijon mustard
Optional: 2-oz. jar chopped
   pimentos, drained
1 c. shredded Cheddar cheese

In a saucepan, cover broccoli with water; cook over medium-high heat until crisp-tender. Drain well; set aside. Meanwhile, unroll dough into 2 long rectangles. Press into an ungreased 13"x9" baking pan, pressing up the sides to form a crust. Bake at 375 degrees for 8 minutes; remove from oven. Scatter broccoli and chicken evenly over crust; set aside. In a large bowl, stir together remaining ingredients except cheese; spoon evenly over chicken. Sprinkle with cheese. Bake, uncovered, at 375 degrees for 15 to 20 minutes, until cheese is melted and bubbly. Let stand 5 minutes; cut into squares. Makes 8 servings.

Hosting a midday brunch? Along with breakfast foods like baked eggs, coffee cake and cereal, offer a light, savory main dish or two for those who have already enjoyed breakfast.

Christmas
Comfort Foods

Orange-Cranberry Oatmeal

Marlene Burns
Swisher, IA

*This oatmeal is fun to make, tasty and ready in 15 minutes or less.
I found the recipe in a folder I inherited from my sister Marlys. She
has passed away, but will be remembered for her great cooking.*

2 c. water
3 T. frozen orange juice
   concentrate
1 c. quick-cooking oats,
   uncooked
1/3 c. toasted wheat germ

1/4 c. dried cranberries
11-oz. can mandarin oranges,
   drained
3 T. brown sugar, packed
Optional: 1/4 c. chopped walnuts

In a large saucepan, bring water and orange juice to a boil. Stir in oats,
wheat germ and cranberries; return to a boil. Cook and stir for 2 minutes.
Remove from heat; stir in remaining ingredients. Makes 4 servings.

Christmas Tea

Amy Butcher
Columbus, GA

*This fruity, spiced tea is perfect for Christmas breakfasts,
holiday parties or a special evening treat.*

10 c. hot brewed black tea
8 c. cranberry juice
1/2 to 1 c. sugar, to taste

20 whole cloves
6 4-inch cinnamon sticks
1 lemon, thinly sliced

In a large stockpot over medium heat, simmer brewed tea, cranberry
juice and sugar until sugar dissolves. Place cloves and cinnamon sticks
in spice bags; add to tea along with lemon. Simmer until heated
through. Serve hot or chilled. Makes 18 servings.

For delicious-smelling spiced
pomanders, use a tapestry needle
to pierce a design into oranges, then
press whole cloves into the holes.
Heap in a bowl and allow to dry.

Cozy Christmas Brunch

Banana Bread Hot Cereal

Donna Acierno
Westminster, CO

One cold winter's day, my husband was getting ready to shovel more than a foot of snow around our Colorado home. I created this breakfast to warm him up before he went out in the cold. He liked it so much that he suggested that I send the recipe to Gooseberry Patch. So, here it is!

1 c. water
1 c. milk
1/3 c. hot wheat cereal, uncooked
1 to 2 ripe bananas, mashed
2 T. dried cranberries
1/8 t. pumpkin pie spice or
    cinnamon

1/8 t. salt
2 T. whipping cream or
    half-and-half
2 to 3 T. chopped pecans
maple syrup or sugar-free syrup
    to taste

In a saucepan over medium heat, bring water and milk to a boil. While whisking, slowly add cereal; reduce heat to medium-low. Keep whisking and add bananas, cranberries, spice and salt. Cook for about 2-1/2 minutes, until thickened. To serve, spoon into 2 bowls. Drizzle with cream or half-and-half; sprinkle with pecans. Add an extra sprinkle of spice, if desired. Sweeten with syrup, as desired. Makes 2 servings.

When vacationing throughout the year, look for Christmas ornaments for your tree. Come December, they're sure to bring great memories of family travels and fun!

Christmas
Comfort Foods

Candied Gingerbread Muffins

Audrey Laudenat
East Haddam, CT

These muffins have been a longtime favorite of our family. I added the crystallized ginger to give them a little more zest...the result was an immediate do-again! A little whipped cream on the side also makes a nice presentation for either brunch or dessert.

2 eggs
3/4 c. brown sugar, packed
3/4 c. molasses
3/4 c. shortening, melted
2-1/3 c. all-purpose flour
1/2 t. baking powder
2 t. baking soda
1/2 t. salt

1-1/4 t. cinnamon
3/4 t. ground ginger
1/2 t. nutmeg
1/ 8 t. ground cloves
1 c. boiling water
1/2 c. crystallized ginger, finely
    chopped and divided
Garnish: whipped cream or butter

Beat eggs in a large bowl; add brown sugar, molasses and shortening. In another bowl, mix flour, baking powder, baking soda, salt and spices; sift into egg mixture and stir hard. Pour in boiling water; mix hard. Gently stir in 1/4 cup crystallized ginger. Pour batter into 6 greased jumbo muffin cups, filling each 2/3 full. Bake at 350 degrees for 45 minutes, or until a toothpick tests clean. (May also use a regular muffin tin; bake for 30 minutes.) Remove from oven; sprinkle with remaining crystallized ginger. Serve warm, topped with whipped cream or butter. Makes 6 jumbo muffins.

Beeswax candles have such a sweet fragrance...wrap up a bundle and tie with a length of wide rick rack for a gift from the heart.

Cozy Christmas
Brunch

Syrniki Russian Pancakes

Ann Farris
Biscoe, AR

*At my workplace, there is a steady stream of all kinds of people.
This recipe came from a former Russian citizen who is now a proud
American citizen. To serve the pancakes the Russian way, top with
sour cream and your favorite fruit preserves.*

16-oz. container farmers' cheese
　or cottage cheese
2 eggs, beaten
1-1/3 c. all-purpose flour,
　divided

1/4 c. sugar
1/2 t salt
6 to 8 T. oil for frying, divided
Garnish: powdered sugar or
　maple syrup

Place cheese in a large bowl; add eggs and mix well. Add 1/2 cup flour
and mix well. Add another 1/2 cup flour, sugar and salt. Mix well, using
a fork to break apart any clumps; set aside. Add remaining flour to a
small bowl. Scoop out 1/4 cup dough; use your hands to flatten dough
into a small patty. Coat pancake with flour on both sides, shaking off
any excess; set aside while making other pancakes. In a large skillet
over medium heat, heat 3 to 4 tablespoons oil. Working in batches,
cook on both sides till golden, adding more oil as needed. To serve,
sprinkle pancakes with powdered sugar or drizzle with maple syrup.
Serves 8.

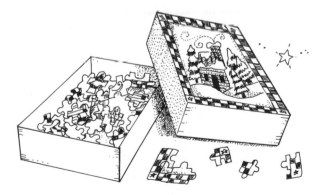

Start a new tradition! Lay out a Christmas-themed jigsaw puzzle
early in December. Family members are sure to enjoy fitting
a few pieces in place whenever they pass by.

Christmas
Comfort Foods

Elizabeth's BLT Pie

Elizabeth Smithson
Mayfield, KY

An old comfort food recipe...can't go wrong with bacon!

3/4 lb. bacon, crisply cooked
   and crumbled
1 c. shredded Swiss cheese
4 eggs, beaten
1-1/2 c. milk
1 c. biscuit baking mix

1/2 c. mayonnaise-style salad
   dressing
1/8 t. salt
1/8 t. pepper
Garnish: shredded lettuce,
   sliced tomatoes

Layer crumbled bacon and cheese in a greased 9" pie plate; set aside. In a large bowl, beat remaining ingredients except garnish until smooth. Pour into pie plate. Bake at 400 degrees for 30 to 35 minutes, until set. Cool for 5 minutes; garnish with lettuce and tomatoes. Cut into wedges. Serves 4 to 6.

Our Favorite Hot Cocoa Mix

Wendy Jo Minotte
Duluth, MN

This is a delicious treat on a cold winter day! I have been making this hot cocoa mix for over 30 years to share with family & friends. For a Christmas gift that's sure to be welcome, add some mini marshmallows and fill a plastic bag with several servings of this cocoa mix. Tuck into a festive mug and top with a colorful bow.

11 c. powdered milk
4 c. chocolate drink mix
1-1/2 c. powdered non-dairy
   creamer

1 c. powdered sugar

Combine all ingredients in a very large bowl; mix thoroughly. Store in an airtight container. To use, place 1/3 cup mix in a mug; add hot water to fill mug and stir well. Makes about 50 servings.

Set out peppermint sticks for stirring breakfast cocoa...it's Christmas!

Cozy Christmas Brunch

Family Favorite Breakfast Casserole

Natalie Swaim
Sullivan, IL

This recipe is a favorite that we enjoy all throughout the year. Most importantly, it's a big part of my husband's family Christmas tradition. Every Christmas morning, we all gather at his parents' house for breakfast and family time, followed by presents by the tree. There is nothing better during the holidays than gathering with family, eating delicious food!

1 lb. ground pork sausage,
    browned and drained
6 slices bread, cubed
1 c. shredded Cheddar cheese

6 eggs, beaten
2 c. milk
1 t. dry mustard
1 t. salt

Combine all ingredients in a large bowl; mix well and transfer to a greased 3-quart casserole dish. Cover and refrigerate for 12 hours or overnight. In the morning, let stand at room temperature for one hour. Bake, uncovered, at 350 degrees for 45 minutes, or until puffy, golden and a knife tip inserted in the center comes out clean. Makes 8 servings.

A Christmas wreath for breakfast! Simply arrange refrigerated cinnamon rolls on a baking sheet in a wreath shape and bake as usual. Spread with frosting, sprinkle with green sugar and decorate with candied cherries.

Christmas
Comfort Foods

All-Time Favorite Pancakes with Berry Syrup

Elisha Nelson
Brookline, MO

My family loves these fluffy pancakes for breakfast or dinner. My little guy loves them shaped into snowmen in the wintertime, or a famous mouse character the rest of the year! We love to top these with warm, fresh homemade Berry Syrup...yummy!

3/4 c. buttermilk
1 egg, beaten
2-1/2 T. sugar
2 T. butter, melted
3/4 c. all-purpose flour

1/4 c. whole-wheat flour
1 t. baking powder
1/2 t. baking soda
1/2 t. salt
oil for frying

In a large bowl, whisk together buttermilk, egg, sugar and butter. Add flours, baking powder, baking soda and salt; whisk just until blended. Heat a skillet to medium-high heat and brush with oil. Pour batter onto skillet by 1/4 cupfuls. Cook until bubbles form and edges begin to turn golden; flip over. Cook on the other side for one to 2 minutes, until golden. Serve with warm Berry Syrup. Serves 4.

Berry Syrup:

1 c. favorite fresh or frozen
　　berries

1/2 c. pure maple syrup
3 T. butter

Combine berries, syrup, and butter in a saucepan. Simmer until berries are soft and tender.

Tie tiny Christmas ornaments onto stemmed glasses with
ribbon bows. So festive for a holiday brunch!

Cozy Christmas Brunch

Spinach Frittata with Feta & Tomatoes

Doreen Knapp
Stanfordville, NY

I make this recipe often. I try to do a really big breakfast as a family on Sundays, and often make it for company at brunch too.

8 eggs
1/3 c. low-fat milk
1 t. Mediterranean seasoning
1/3 c. onion, chopped
1/3 c. green pepper, chopped

1/2 c. tomato, chopped
2 c. fresh spinach, torn
1 T. olive oil or avocado oil
1/3 c. crumbled feta cheese

Beat eggs in a large bowl. Whisk in milk and seasoning; stir in onion, pepper, tomato and spinach. Brush a cast-iron skillet with oil; pour egg mixture into skillet. Bake, uncovered, at 350 degrees for 25 to 35 minutes, until set. Remove from oven; sprinkle with cheese and cut into wedges. Makes 4 servings.

Start a Christmas scrapbook that you can update every year...
a family photo taken in front of the tree, the children's letters
to Santa, notes on favorite gifts received and special visitors.
Set it out for family & friends to enjoy looking at it. Sure to
make for many smiles over the years!

Christmas
Comfort Foods

Creme Brulee French Toast Bake

Tracy Pellegrin
Norco, LA

My kids and grandkids love this casserole on Christmas morning. I love that I can assemble it the night before! I let it come to room temperature while we open presents, and then pop it in the oven while I prep the other breakfast items.

1/2 c. butter
1 c. brown sugar, packed
2 T. corn syrup
9-inch round loaf challah bread
5 eggs

1-1/2 c. half-and-half
1/4 t. salt
1 t. vanilla extract
Optional: 1 t. orange-flavored
    liqueur

In a small saucepan over medium heat, melt butter with brown sugar and corn syrup, stirring until smooth. Pour into a greased 13"x9" baking pan; set aside. Cut 6, one-inch slices from center portion of loaf; trim crusts. (Reserve any remaining bread for another use.) Arrange bread slices in one layer in pan, squeezing them slightly to fit; set aside. In a large bowl, whisk together eggs, half-and-half, salt, vanilla and liqueur, if using. Pour evenly over bread. Cover and chill at least 8 hours and up to one day. For serving, bring bread mixture to room temperature. Bake, uncovered, at 350 degrees on center rack of oven for 35 to 40 minutes, until puffed and edges are pale golden. Serves 8 to 10.

For a thoughtful gift that's easy on the wallet, purchase a calendar
and fill in birthdays, anniversaries and other important
family events. A nice gift for those new to the family!

Cozy Christmas Brunch

Quick Coconut Toast

Marsha Baker
Pioneer, OH

I've been making this breakfast treat for decades, since my kids were small. It's quick and oh-so tasty...a family favorite.

1/2 c. butter, melted
2/3 to 1 c. sugar
1 c. unsweetened flaked coconut

1 t. vanilla extract
1 egg, beaten
9 to 10 slices bread

In a small bowl, combine butter and sugar; stir in coconut and vanilla. Add egg, blending well; mixture will be thick. Spread mixture generously over each slice of bread. Arrange slices on ungreased baking sheets. Bake at 350 degrees for 15 to 18 minutes, until lightly golden. Makes 4 to 5 servings.

Egg & Potato Pie

Wendy Jacobs
Idaho Falls, ID

A hearty hot breakfast that goes together in a jiffy!

3 c. frozen shredded hashbrown
   potatoes, thawed and
   patted dry
1/4 c. butter, melted
3 eggs, beaten

1/2 c. milk
1/2 c. sour cream
1-1/2 c. shredded sharp Cheddar
   cheese
4 green onions, sliced

Place hashbrowns in a bowl; drizzle with butter and mix lightly. Press into the bottom and up the sides of a 9" pie plate. Bake at 375 degrees for 20 minutes, or until golden. Meanwhile, in another bowl, whisk eggs and milk until blended. Stir in sour cream, cheese and onions; spoon into crust. Decrease oven temperature to 350 degrees. Bake for 30 minutes, or until center is set and crust is golden. Let stand 5 minutes; cut into wedges. Makes 6 servings.

A fringed red plaid throw makes a festive runner
for a brunch table.

Christmas Comfort Foods

Toffee, Pecan & Caramel Scones

Elizabeth McCord
Memphis, TN

Tea parties are a favorite around our house! And scones are a star at any tea party. These scones combine three of our favorite things... toffee, pecans and caramel. The result? Delightfully perfect scones.

2 c. all-purpose flour
2 T. sugar
2 t. baking powder
1/2 t. baking soda
1/4 t. salt
1/2 c. cold butter, cubed

1 egg, beaten
1/2 c. milk
1/2 c. toffee baking bits
1/2 c. caramel baking bits
1/3 c. chopped pecans

In a bowl, combine flour, sugar, baking powder, baking soda and salt. Whisk together until thoroughly combined. Cut butter into flour mixture with 2 knives or a pastry cutter until crumbly. Gently stir in egg and milk. Add remaining ingredients except pecans; stir just until combined. Place dough on a floured surface; gently pat out to about one inch thick. Using a pizza cutter or a knife, cut into triangles or circles. Place on a greased baking sheet. Bake at 350 degrees for 13 to 15 minutes, just until golden on the bottoms. Remove to a wire rack; cool completely. Drizzle with Caramel Drizzle; sprinkle with pecans. Makes one dozen.

Caramel Drizzle:

1/2 c. caramel baking bits

1/4 c. whipping cream or milk

Add caramel bits to a microwave-safe bowl. Microwave at 30-second intervals until melted. Gently whisk in cream or milk, stirring until smooth.

Devon Cream is scrumptious on scones. Blend together 3 ounces softened cream cheese, one tablespoon sugar and 1/8 teaspoon salt. Beat in a cup of whipping cream until stiff peaks form and chill.

Comfort in a Soup Bowl

Christmas Comfort Foods

Supper Soup Italiano

Virginia Campbell
Clifton Forge, VA

I make soup and bread just about every weekend during fall and winter. This hearty sausage and vegetable soup is made even more savory and satisfying by the addition of cheese tortellini.

1-1/2 lbs. hot or mild Italian
    pork sausage links, removed
    from casings
4 c. beef or chicken broth
28-oz. can Italian-style crushed
    tomatoes in purée
1 c. onion, chopped
12-oz. pkg. frozen broccoli,
    cauliflower & carrot blend

1/2 t. garlic powder
1 to 2 bay leaves
salt and pepper to taste
16-oz. pkg. refrigerated or frozen
    cheese tortellini, uncooked
Garnish: croutons, shredded
    Parmesan cheese

Brown sausage in a large skillet over medium heat, breaking up chunks. Drain; transfer to a stockpot or Dutch oven. Add remaining ingredients except tortellini and garnish; reduce heat to medium-low. Simmer for 45 minutes to one hour, stirring occasionally, until vegetables are tender. Add tortellini to pan; cook according to time given on package directions. May also combine browned sausage and remaining ingredients in a slow cooker; cover and cook on low setting for 6 to 9 hours. Add cooked tortellini in the last 15 minutes. At serving time, discard bay leaves; top with croutons and Parmesan cheese. Makes 8 to 10 servings.

Create a special food tradition to enjoy each year as your family trims the tree. Whether it's a buffet of finger foods and spiced cider, sugar cookies and hot cocoa or something else of your own choosing, you'll be making heartfelt memories together.

Comfort in a Soup Bowl

Creamy Root Vegetable Soup

Tiffany Jones
Batesville, AR

One cold day, I was in the mood for something comforting, something I could enjoy in front of the fireplace cuddled under a plaid throw blanket. This slow-cooker soup hit the spot!

6 potatoes, peeled and cubed
3 carrots, peeled and cubed
3 parsnips, peeled and cubed
1 onion, diced
14-1/2 oz. can diced tomatoes
　　with green chiles
10-3/4 oz. can cream of
　　celery soup
10-3/4 oz. can roasted red
　　pepper soup
10-3/4 oz. can cream of
　　mushroom soup
32-oz. container vegetable broth
salt and pepper to taste
8-oz. pkg. pasteurized process
　　cheese spread, cubed

In a 6-quart slow cooker, combine all ingredients except cheese; mix gently. Cover and cook on high setting for 6 to 7 hours, until hot and bubbly. Add cheese; continue cooking for 30 minutes. Stir again and serve. Makes 6 to 8 servings.

Slow cookers come in so many sizes, you might want to have more than one! A 4-quart size is handy for a family of 4, while a 5-1/2 to 6-quart one is just right for larger families and potlucks. Just have room for one? Choose an oval slow cooker... roasts and whole chickens will fit perfectly.

Christmas
Comfort Foods

Mom's Poor Man's Soup

Barbara White
Thompson, OH

My mom always made this hearty soup and it was a family favorite. It is so easy and good. My mom always called it Beadleman's Soup. I never knew what beadleman's meant, but I think it probably means "poor man's." It's so good on a cold winter's day. I don't have a written recipe, so I made it from memory. Any leftover vegetables you have on hand can be added.

1 lb. ground beef
2 t. oil
6 c. beef broth or water
14-1/2 oz. can diced tomatoes
1 c. canned or frozen corn
1 onion, chopped

2 carrots, peeled and chopped
2 stalks celery, chopped
2 bay leaves
salt and pepper to taste
1/2 to 1 c. long-cooking rice or
    barley, uncooked

Brown beef in a soup pot with a little oil; drain. Add beef broth or water, tomatoes with juice, remaining vegetables and bay leaves. Bring to a boil; reduce heat to low. Simmer until vegetables are soft; season with salt and pepper. Add desired amount rice or barley, depending on how thick you want the soup to be; simmer until tender. Discard bay leaves before serving. Makes 4 to 6 servings.

Crisp, savory saltine crackers are a must with steamy bowls of soup! In a large bowl, mix 1/4 cup olive oil and 1/4 cup grated Parmesan cheese; add a sleeve of saltines. Toss to coat well and lay on a baking sheet. Bake at 300 degrees for 15 minutes, or until golden.

Comfort in a Soup Bowl

Buttermilk Biscuits

Beckie Apple
Grannis, AR

I made my first biscuits when I was ten years old...that was over 50 years ago! These buttermilk biscuits are always a requirement for our holiday breakfast table.

3 c. self-rising flour, divided
3 T. sugar
2 T. baking powder

1/4 c. margarine, diced
3/4 c. buttermilk
2 T. oil

In a large bowl, combine 2-1/2 cups flour, sugar and baking powder; mix thoroughly. Add margarine pieces. With your fingers or a pastry cutter, crumble margarine into flour until only small fragments remain. Add buttermilk and stir until combined. Add oil; using a spatula, scrape the sides of bowl until dough comes together in a ball. Spread remaining flour on work surface. Roll out dough to about 1/2-inch thickness. Cut out biscuits with a biscuit cutter. Arrange biscuits on a baking sheet coated with non-stick vegetable spray. Bake at 400 degrees for 25 minutes, or until golden. Makes about 10 biscuits.

If you have treasured handwritten recipes, photocopy them to share with family. It's so heartwarming to see your favorites in Grandma's own handwriting.

Christmas Comfort Foods

White Bean Chicken Soup

Kimberly Hancock
Murrieta, CA

Soups are my love language...I could eat soup every day! This slow-cooker soup is so delicious. It's hearty & comforting, perfect for chilly fall and winter nights. It's even great for busy days, because it can be started in the afternoon and be ready by dinnertime. It also freezes really well.

4 boneless, skinless chicken
  breasts
1-1/2 c. carrots, peeled and diced
1-1/2 c. celery, diced
1 c. yellow onion, diced
3 cloves garlic, minced
14-1/2 oz. can diced tomatoes
2 15-1/2 oz. cans cannellini
  beans, drained and rinsed
32-oz. container chicken or
  vegetable broth

kosher salt and pepper to taste
1 t. dried oregano
1 t. dried thyme
1 t. dried basil
1/2 t. red pepper flakes
2 bay leaves
1 sprig fresh rosemary
Optional: shredded Parmesan
  cheese

In a 6-quart slow cooker, combine chicken, carrots, celery, onion and garlic. Add tomatoes with juice and beans; pour in broth. Season generously with salt and pepper; add remaining seasonings. Stir together well. Cover and cook on high setting for 3 to 4 hours, or on low setting for 6 to 8 hours, until chicken is cooked through. Discard bay leaves and rosemary sprig. Use 2 forks to shred chicken; stir into soup and serve, topped with Parmesan cheese if desired. Serves 8.

Make a double batch of soup to freeze for later! To save freezer space, divide cooled soup into plastic freezer bags, seal and lay bags flat on a baking sheet in the freezer. Once frozen, remove the baking sheet. Thaw overnight in the fridge, or even in the microwave anytime it's needed.

Comfort in a Soup Bowl

Creamy Pea Soup

Julie Ann Perkins
Anderson, IN

A wonderful fresh flavor to start off your meal, or a warm soup with fresh bread & butter for a delicious meal. Shared in memory of my brother Jeff, who loved pea soup growing up! You could add diced ham to make it more hearty.

2 T. butter
1 T. chopped onion
2 c. frozen peas
1/2 t. sugar

2 c. water
1 c. whipping cream
salt and pepper to taste

Melt butter in a large saucepan over medium heat. Add onion; cook and stir until translucent. Add peas, sugar and water; cover and cook until peas are tender. Transfer to a blender or food processor; process until puréed. Return to pan; add cream, salt and pepper. Heat through and serve. Makes 4 servings.

Broccoli-Cheese Soup

Lisa Smith
Huntington, IN

Given to me by my best friend, this slow-cooker recipe is always delicious. Very easy to double, too!

10-3/4 oz. can cream of
    mushroom soup
10-oz. pkg. frozen chopped
    broccoli, thawed

6 slices American cheese,
    chopped
1-1/4 c. whole or 2% milk

Combine all ingredients in a 3-quart slow cooker, adding milk to desired consistency. Cover and cook on low setting for 4 to 5 hours, stirring once or twice to melt the cheese. Makes 4 servings.

A cheery, painted chalkboard is ideal for kids as they count down the days until Christmas.

Christmas Comfort Foods

Italian Sausage & Tomato Soup
Louise Soweski
Woodbridge, NJ

I've always loved the taste of sausage and tomato together in a recipe. One day I wanted to cook a warm and hearty soup. I had all the ingredients on hand, so one by one, into the pot they went. The result was this delicious soup for a cold winter's night. I hope you enjoy it just as much as I do.

1 t. olive oil
16-oz. pkg. ground turkey
   sausage
1 large onion, cut into chunks
4 cloves garlic, chopped
1/8 t. Italian seasoning
salt and pepper to taste
2 carrots, peeled and thinly sliced

14-1/2 oz. can diced tomatoes
15-1/2 oz. can cannellini beans,
   drained and rinsed
14-1/2 oz. can beef broth
14-1/2 oz. can chicken broth
6-1/2 oz. can tomato sauce
2 bay leaves
1 c. small soup pasta, uncooked

Heat olive oil in a large pot over medium heat. Add sausage; cook and stir until lightly browned, about 5 minutes. Add onion and garlic; cook and stir until onion is tender, about 5 minutes. Season with Italian seasoning, salt and pepper. Stir in carrots; cook and stir until beginning to soften, 5 to 7 minutes. Add tomatoes with juice, beans, broths and tomato sauce; stir in bay leaves. Continue to simmer until carrots are tender, about 5 minutes. Add pasta; cook and stir until pasta is cooked through but firm to the bite. Discard bay leaves before serving. Makes 6 to 8 servings.

Christmas bazaars are so much fun! Jot down the dates on your calendar and invite girlfriends to come along.

Comfort in a
Soup Bowl

30-Minute Dinner Rolls

Ann Farris
Biscoe, AR

Need some hot rolls in a hurry? Don't fret...here you go!

1 c. plus 2 T. very warm water,
   110 to 115 degrees
2 T. active dry yeast
1/3 c. olive oil
1/4 c. sugar

3-1/2 c. bread flour or all-
   purpose flour, divided
1/2 t. salt
1 egg, beaten
Garnish: melted butter

In the bowl of an electric mixer, combine warm water, yeast, oil and sugar. Let stand for 10 minutes to allow yeast to bloom; mixture will look puffy. Add 2 cups flour, salt and egg. Beat with mixer on medium speed, using a dough hook; gradually beat in remaining flour. Allow mixer to do the work, kneading it all together until dough becomes a soft, smooth ball. Shape dough into 12 balls; place in a greased 13"x9" baking pan. Let stand for 10 minutes. Bake at 400 degrees for 10 minutes, or just until tops are golden. Remove from oven; brush tops with melted butter. Makes one dozen.

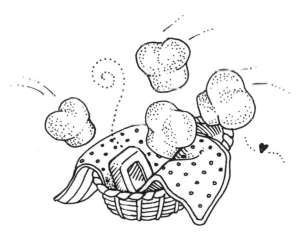

Keep rolls nice and warm as you enjoy your soup. Before arranging rolls in a bread basket, place a terra cotta warming tile in the bottom and line with a Christmasy tea towel.

Christmas
Comfort Foods

Spanish Bean Soup

Ronda Morhaime
Rogersville, TN

This recipe is taken from my time in Spain. One of my next-door neighbors made it often. I've changed it just a little so that I could use ingredients from our local grocery. Saffron is expensive, but turmeric can be used in a pinch. Serve with warm crusty bread...so satisfying.

1 T. extra-virgin olive oil
3/4 c. yellow onion, chopped
6 cloves garlic, chopped
1/2 lb. Spanish chorizo pork
    sausage, casings removed,
    halved and thinly sliced
1/2 lb. cooked ham steak, cut
    into 1/2-inch cubes

6 c. low-sodium chicken broth
3 15-1/2 oz. cans white beans,
    drained and rinsed
4 green onions, thinly sliced
1 t. saffron threads or turmeric
kosher salt and pepper to taste
3 bay leaves

Heat olive oil in a Dutch oven over medium heat. Add onion; sauté until translucent. Add garlic; sauté for 30 seconds, or until fragrant. Add sausage; cook until browned. Add ham; brown lightly. Add remaining ingredients and bring to a boil. Reduce heat to medium-low. Simmer for 45 minutes, stirring occasionally. Discard bay leaves before serving. Makes 8 servings.

Keep all of your family's favorite holiday story books in a basket by a cozy chair. Set aside one night as family night to read your favorites together.

Comfort in a
Soup Bowl

Corn Chowder with Bacon

Tina Vawter
Sheridan, IN

A chilly-weather family favorite...it's one of our comfort foods.
Sometimes I'll add a little extra bacon...can't have too much!

8 slices bacon, diced
1 c. onion, chopped
4 14-1/2 oz. cans chicken broth
4 c. creamed corn

4 c. potatoes, peeled and diced
salt and pepper to taste
Garnish: chopped fresh parsley

Cook bacon in a Dutch oven over medium heat until almost crisp. Add onion and cook until tender; drain drippings, if desired. Add chicken broth, corn and potatoes; cover and bring to a boil. Reduce heat to medium-low. Simmer 12 to 15 minutes, until potatoes are tender. Add salt and pepper to taste; garnish with parsley. Serves 8.

Lentil Soup with Dumplings

Trudy Gernert
Seymour, IN

This is delicious, and so simple to make! My mother-in-law gave me
this recipe when I married. It's one of my husband's favorites.

7 c. water
1 c. onion, chopped
1 meaty ham hock, or
    2 c. cooked ham, diced

16-oz. pkg. dried lentils, rinsed
    and sorted
2 12-oz. pkgs. frozen
    dumplings, uncooked

In a soup kettle, combine all ingredients except dumplings. Bring to a boil over high heat; reduce heat to medium-low and simmer for one hour. Add dumplings while soup is boiling; stir well. Cook according to time given on package directions. If using ham bone, cut off ham and return to soup. Ladle into bowls and serve. Makes 5 to 7 servings.

Take a walk on Christmas Eve and look
for the Christmas star.

Tempting Tomato Soup

Becky Bosen
Layton, UT

This soup is perfect in the crisp fall or snowy wintertime.
It's super quick to make. Paired with grilled cheese sandwiches
or crusty bread, it's sure to warm your tummy!

28-oz. can petite diced tomatoes
32-oz. container chicken broth
2 t. sugar
2 t. fresh basil, chopped,
   or 1 t. dried basil
1 t. dried oregano

1 t. salt
1 t. pepper
8-oz. container whipping cream
2 t. cornstarch
2 t. cold water

In a saucepan, combine tomatoes with juice, chicken broth, sugar, herbs and seasonings. Bring to a boil over high heat. Carefully pour mixture into a blender; process until smooth and return to saucepan. Stir in cream; reduce heat to medium-low. In a cup, mix cornstarch with cold water; stir into soup. Simmer for 10 to 15 minutes. Makes 6 to 8 servings.

Try something new...grilled cheese croutons! Make grilled cheese
sandwiches as usual, then cut them into small squares.
Toss into a bowl of creamy tomato soup...yum!

Comfort in a Soup Bowl

Granny's Vegetable Soup

Jenny Bishoff
Oakland, MD

My granny made a similar soup for family reunions and gatherings over the years. With the more recent addition of riced cauliflower, it's even more nutritious.

1-1/2 lbs. ground beef
1 t. garlic powder
1 t. onion powder
1 t. salt
46-oz. bottle vegetable cocktail juice

16-oz. pkg. frozen mixed vegetables
12-oz. pkg. frozen riced cauliflower
2 cubes beef bouillon
2 c. water

In a soup pot over medium heat, brown beef with seasonings; drain. Add remaining ingredients; mix well. Cover and simmer for one hour, stirring occasionally. May also combine all ingredients in a 6 quart slow cooker; cover and cook on low setting for 4 to 6 hours. Makes 8 servings.

Traveling for the holidays? No worries! Have little ones leave Santa a note at your home, with instructions telling him where you'll be visiting the night before Christmas.

Christmas
Comfort Foods

Sausage & White Bean Soup

JoAnn
Gooseberry Patch

We enjoy this hearty soup with toasted baguettes for dipping...yum!

2 T. olive oil
1-1/2 lbs. Italian pork sausage
   links
2 carrots, peeled and diced
2 onions, diced

2 stalks celery, diced
1 t. dried thyme
3 15-1/2 oz. cans cannellini
   beans, divided
4 c. chicken broth

Heat oil in a large stockpot over medium heat. Brown sausages; remove to a plate and cool for 5 minutes. Add carrots, onions, celery and thyme to pan; sauté for 10 minutes. Process one can of beans in a blender until puréed; add to pan. Slice sausages thinly; add to pan along with chicken broth and remaining beans. Simmer over medium-low heat for 20 minutes. Makes 8 servings.

Baked Potato Soup

Brenda Bodnar
Mayfield Village, OH

I tossed this soup together after Christmas with leftovers on hand. My family urged me to write it down so I could make it again!

1/2 c. onion, diced
1 T. butter
2 c. Yukon Gold potatoes, diced
2 c. shredded sharp Cheddar
   cheese

4 c. chicken broth
1/2 c. half-and-half
1/2 lb. bacon, diced and crisply
   cooked

In a large skillet over low heat, sauté onion in butter for 5 minutes. Add potatoes; cook another 5 minutes. Add cheese and chicken broth; cook and stir until melted. Add half-and-half and bacon; heat through just until hot. Serve in mugs. Makes 4 servings.

Christmas is the family time, the good time of the year.
–Samuel Johnson

Comfort in a
Soup Bowl

Meatballs & Veggies Cheese Soup
Denise Webb
Guyton, GA

This is such a great comforting soup on all those busy, cold days of winter. Serve with a hearty country-style bread.

1 lb. ground beef
1/4 c. soft bread crumbs
1 egg, beaten
1/2 t. hot pepper sauce
1/2 t. salt
2 c. water
1 c. celery, chopped

1/2 c. onion, chopped
2 cubes beef bouillon
1 c. canned or frozen corn
1 c. potatoes, peeled and sliced
1/2 c. carrots, peeled and sliced
16-oz. jar pasteurized process
  cheese dip

In a bowl, mix together beef, bread crumbs, egg, hot sauce and salt. Roll into small balls; place in a 5-quart slow cooker. Add remaining ingredients except cheese. Cover and cook on low setting for 8 to 10 hours. Just before serving, stir in cheese. Serves 6 to 8.

Fill pint-size canning jars with red cinnamon candies and nestle a votive candle in the center. They'll look so welcoming, lined up along the center of the dinner table.

Christmas
Comfort Foods

Hearty Italian Butternut Squash Soup

Margaret Welder
Madrid, IA

Winter squash has always been a favorite of mine and I look for new ways to serve it. I made up this recipe after seeing one for a Middle Eastern squash soup. A spicy Italian sausage will make the soup spicy, which I like, while my husband likes a milder version.

1 lb. ground spicy or mild Italian pork sausage
1-1/2 c. onions, diced
1 red pepper, diced
4 cloves garlic, minced
3 c. butternut squash, peeled and cubed
2 14-1/2 oz. cans chicken broth
16-oz. can Great Northern beans, drained
14-1/2 oz. can petite diced tomatoes
1 T. tomato paste
1 T. chicken bouillon granules
1/2 t. paprika
1 T. fresh basil, minced, or 1 t. dried basil
1 t. fresh oregano, minced, or 1/2 t. dried oregano
2 T. fresh parsley, minced, or 1 t. dried parsley
1/2 t. salt
1/4 t. pepper
Optional: sour cream or plain yogurt

In a soup pot over medium heat, brown and crumble sausage; drain. Add onions and red pepper; cook until nearly tender. Add garlic; cook briefly. Add remaining ingredients except optional sour cream or yogurt; stir to combine. Bring to a simmer; reduce heat to low and cook until squash is tender, about 20 minutes. Serve topped with sour cream or yogurt, if desired. Makes 8 to 10 servings.

Chill December brings the sleet,
Blazing fire, and Christmas treat.

–Sara Coleridge

Comfort in a
Soup Bowl

Cloverleaf Rolls

Charity Hullinger
Leon, IA

You'll be proud to serve these easy-to-make rolls! They're best enjoyed the same day they are made.

1 env. quick-rise yeast
1-1/3 c. milk, warmed to
   110 to 115 degrees
3 c. all-purpose flour, divided
3 T. olive oil

1 T. sugar
1 t. salt
2 T. butter, melted and divided
coarse sea salt to taste

In the bowl of an electric mixer, dissolve yeast in warm milk. Stir in one cup flour; beat on medium speed until smooth. Stir in remaining flour; add oil, sugar, and salt. Beat on low speed until a soft dough forms. If necessary, add a little more flour to make a soft dough. Cover and let rise in warm place until double in size, about 45 minutes. Coat 12 muffin cups with one tablespoon melted butter; set aside. Punch down dough in the center; fold over a couple times. Pinch dough into one-inch balls; quickly roll in the center of your palms. Add 3 balls to each muffin cup; brush with remaining butter and sprinkle with sea salt. Bake at 400 degrees for 15 minutes, or until edges are lightly golden. Best served the same day. Makes one dozen.

Garlic-Chive Bread

Gladys Kielar
Whitehouse, OH

Dress up a loaf of bread deliciously in just minutes!

1/4 c. butter, softened
1/4 c. grated Parmesan cheese
2 T. fresh chives, snipped

1 clove garlic, minced
1 loaf French bread, cut into
   1-inch slices

Blend butter, Parmesan cheese, chives and garlic in a bowl. Spread mixture on one side of each slice of bread; reassemble loaf on a large piece of heavy-duty aluminum foil. Seal edges of foil; place on a baking sheet. Bake at 350 degrees for 25 to 30 minutes, until heated through. Serves 6.

Christmas Comfort Foods

Cami's Super-Easy Chili

Cami Seager
Ashburn, VA

My family loves this recipe, especially in the fall and winter months.
They always request it! We like it with warm cornbread.

1-1/2 to 2 lbs. ground beef
1 c. onion, chopped
2 14-1/2 oz. cans diced tomatoes
4 15-1/2 oz. cans chili beans,
   drained
1 c. catsup
1/4 c. sugar

2 T. vinegar
1 t. dried oregano
1/2 t. chili powder
2 t. salt
1 t. seasoned pepper
Garnish: shredded Cheddar
   cheese

In a soup pot over medium heat, cook beef and onion until beef is no
longer pink; drain. Stir in tomatoes with juice and remaining ingredients
except garnish. Bring to a boil, reduce heat to low and simmer for
30 minutes. Ladle into bowls; top with shredded cheese. Makes 6 to
8 servings.

Soups and stews stay bubbly and warm when spooned into a
slow cooker turned to the low setting. This way, no matter
when family, friends or neighbors arrive for a visit,
the soup will be ready to enjoy.

Comfort in a
Soup Bowl

Mom's Skillet Cornbread

Vanessa Snow
Havelock, NC

As far back as I can remember, the women in our family have used cast-iron skillets for just about everything. You receive a seasoned skillet as a wedding gift, and you use it all your life. Be sure to set out your butter while the cornbread is baking...you'll have nice soft butter to spread on it.

2 8-1/2 oz. pkgs. corn
   muffin mix
1 c. creamed corn
1/3 to 2/3 c. milk

1 egg, beaten
1/2 t. sugar
2 T. bacon drippings

In a bowl, stir together dry muffin mix, corn, 1/3 cup milk, egg and sugar. Batter should be thick, not soupy. If too thick, add remaining milk; set aside. With 2 paper towels, rub the inside of a cast-iron skillet with bacon drippings. Set aside paper towels; pour batter into skillet. Bake at 350 degrees for 20 minutes. Cover warm bread with reserved paper towels, or brush with a little butter. Cut into wedges. Leftovers will keep up to 2 days in a plastic zipping bag, or may be frozen up to 2 months. Makes 6 to 8 servings.

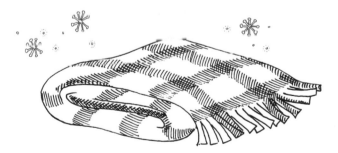

Whip up cozy throws in bright-colored fleece...there are lots of fun choices at the fabric store! Simply snip fringe all around the edges of a 2-yard length of fleece. So easy, you can make one for each member of the family in no time at all.

Christmas Comfort Foods

Chicken & Wild Rice Soup

Courtney Stultz
Weir, KS

This soup is the ultimate comfort food at our house. It is filling, chock-full of veggies and flavor. It also freezes well! We like to make a double batch and freeze some for those cold, busy winter nights. To save time, grab a rotisserie chicken from the store and shred it.

2 c. cooked chicken, shredded
1 c. wild rice, uncooked
2 c. kale or spinach, chopped
1 c. carrots, peeled and diced
1 c. onion, diced
1/2 c. celery, diced
1/2 c. mushrooms, diced

2 cloves garlic, minced
3 c. chicken broth
1 c. regular or dairy-free milk
1 t. dried thyme
1 t. dried parsley
1 t. sea salt
1 t. pepper

In a large stockpot over medium-low heat, combine all ingredients. Cover and cook for 30 to 40 minutes, stirring occasionally, until rice is tender and vegetables are cooked through. Makes 6 servings.

Quick Chicken Noodle Soup

Linda Pitzer
LaPlata, MD

I needed a quick dinner for my granddaughters while their mother was in the hospital having their sister. We ran into the grocery store and came out with four ingredients. Here they are, and everybody loved it! You can add herbs like thyme, rosemary and/or sage if you like, but I didn't, and we all enjoyed it.

1 deli rotisserie chicken
2 32-oz. containers chicken
  bone broth
16-oz. pkg. frozen mixed
  vegetables

2 4-oz. pkgs. chicken noodle
  soup mix

Cut chicken into bite-size pieces, discarding skin and bones. Add chicken and chicken broth to a large soup pot; bring to a boil over medium-high heat. Add vegetables; bring to a boil again. Stir in soup mix. Simmer over medium heat until vegetables and noodles are done, about 15 minutes. Serves 6.

Comfort in a
Soup Bowl

Delightful Sherry Mushroom Potage

Amy Daily
Morrisville, PA

I make this very rich and creamy soup all year 'round. My husband and I enjoy it with a crusty French baguette and a good movie! I like to use half white button mushrooms and half Baby Bellas. If you wish, you can cut the calories and fat by using fat-free half and-half.

2 T. butter
1 t. olive oil
3/4 c. onion, chopped
16-oz. pkg. sliced mushrooms
1/4 c. fresh parsley, finely
    chopped
1 clove garlic, minced
1 t. dried thyme
4 c. chicken broth

4 c. half-and-half
2 c. whipping cream
1 T. sugar
1 t. salt
1/4 t. pepper
3 T. cornstarch
1/2 c. golden sherry or
    chicken broth

In a large stockpot over medium-high heat, melt butter with oil. Add onion, mushrooms, parsley, garlic and thyme. Sauté until mushrooms are softened. Add chicken broth, half-and-half and cream; bring to a boil. Reduce heat to medium; add sugar, salt and pepper. In a small bowl, dissolve cornstarch in sherry or additional chicken broth; add to soup. Cook, stirring constantly, until soup is thickened. Serves 6 to 8.

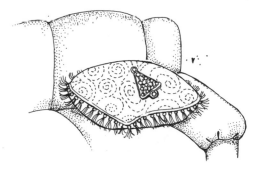

Just for fun, show off favorite vintage Christmas tree brooches! Pin them onto a velvet cushion and tuck into the corner of the sofa.

Christmas Comfort Foods

Angela's Taco Soup

Angela Leers
Taylorville, IL

I love this recipe...you can add just about anything to it! I also mix up the meat. Sometimes I add spicy sausage to the beef, or other times, I will add ground chicken or turkey. It's sooo easy!

1-1/2 lbs. ground beef
1 onion, chopped
2 15-1/2 oz. cans kidney beans
2 14-1/2 oz. cans diced tomatoes
15-1/2 oz. can chili beans
14-1/2 oz. can corn
8-oz. can tomato sauce
4-oz. can diced green chiles
1 c. water

1-1/4 oz. pkg. taco
   seasoning mix
1-oz. pkg. ranch salad
   dressing mix
Garnish: shredded Cheddar
   cheese, sour cream, sliced
   green onions, tortilla or
   corn chips

Brown beef with onion in a large skillet over medium heat; drain. Transfer beef to a soup pot. Add remaining ingredients except garnish; do not drain cans. Stir well; simmer for 15 to 20 minutes, until heated through. May also combine all ingredients in a slow cooker; cover and cook on high setting for 3 hours, or on low setting for 8 hours. At serving time, set out favorite toppings so everyone can garnish their own bowls. Serves 8.

Watch tag sales for a big red speckled enamelware stockpot. It's just the right size for cooking up a family-size batch of soup, with a touch of Christmas cheer.

Comfort in a
Soup Bowl

Real Texas Chili

JonCarole Gilbreath
Tyler, TX

This is just about the most delicious chili in the world! Best when made 24 hours before serving, so the flavors can develop. Sometimes, instead of all lean ground beef, I will use two pounds beef plus a pound of ground hot or mild pork sausage. This chili freezes well...great for enchiladas too!

3 lbs. lean ground beef
1 c. all-purpose flour
2 T. salt
2 T. pepper
1-1/2 c. onions, chopped
3 T. garlic, minced
8 c. hot water

2 8-oz. cans tomato sauce
6 T. chili powder
4 T. paprika
2 T. ground cumin
1 t. sugar
1 t. cayenne pepper or hot pepper
   sauce, or to taste

Place beef in a large bowl; set aside. In a small bowl, combine flour, salt and pepper; add to beef and work together until all the flour is worked into the beef. Sauté beef in a large heavy stockpot over medium-low heat until beef begins to change color. Add onions and garlic; cook until beef is no longer pink but not yet brown, stirring often. Add hot water and simmer for one hour, stirring occasionally. Add remaining ingredients and simmer for another hour, stirring often. Season with more salt, pepper, cayenne or hot sauce, as desired. Makes 12 to 16 servings.

December is packed with decorating, baking and shopping, so take it easy with simple, hearty meals. Make double batches of family favorites like chili or Sloppy Joes early in the holiday season and freeze half to heat and eat later. You'll be so glad you did!

Christmas Comfort Foods

Mom's Chicken & Dumpling Soup

*Laura Witham
Anchorage, AK*

*Whenever we kids weren't feeling well, Mom would make this soup
for us. It was our favorite...we'd always fight over the dumplings!
This recipe is easy to adjust for more dumplings.*

3 T. extra-virgin olive oil
1 onion, diced
4 stalks celery, chopped
2 to 3 carrots, peeled and
   chopped
4 cloves garlic, minced
4 t. dried dill weed

2 bay leaves
salt and pepper to taste
2-1/2 lb. deli rotisserie chicken,
   shredded and bones
   discarded
8 c. chicken broth

Heat oil in a stockpot over medium-high heat; add vegetables and
seasonings. Cook until tender, about 2 to 3 minutes; stir in chicken and
chicken broth. Bring to a boil; reduce heat to a simmer over medium-low
heat. Make dough for Dumplings; add dough to soup by spoonfuls.
Cook for about 5 minutes, until all the dumplings are floating on top.
If not serving right away, turn down to a low simmer. The longer
soup simmers, the better. Discard bay leaves at serving time. Makes
6 servings.

Dumplings:

2 c. all-purpose flour
1 egg, beaten

1-1/2 t. salt, or to taste
1 to 1-1/2 c. milk

Mix all ingredients, adding more or less milk as needed. Dough should
be thick enough to spoon into soup, but not as thick as biscuit dough.

As winter evenings turn dark,
light a candle at the family dinner
table. It'll make an ordinary
meal seem special!

Comfort in a
Soup Bowl

Jam Muffins

Kathy Grashoff
Fort Wayne, IN

You probably already have the ingredients on hand to make a batch of these yummy muffins! Perfect for a snack or alongside soup.

2-1/2 c. all-purpose flour
1/2 c. sugar
1 T. baking powder
1/2 t. salt
1 egg, beaten

1 c. milk
1/2 c. butter, melted
1 t. vanilla extract
1/4 c. favorite jam or preserves

In a large bowl, whisk together flour, sugar, baking powder and salt; set aside. In another bowl, whisk together egg, milk, melted butter and vanilla. Add egg mixture to flour mixture; stir until combined. Batter will be thick. Set aside 1/4 cup batter. Spoon remaining batter into 12 greased muffin cups, filling 1/3 full. Drop one teaspoon jam or preserves into each muffin cup; top each with one teaspoon remaining batter. (There's no need to cover the jam; you aren't trying to seal it in.) Bake at 400 degrees for 20 to 25 minutes, until a toothpick inserted near the center tests clean. Cool slightly; turn muffins out of pan and cool on a wire rack. Makes one dozen.

The best of all gifts around any Christmas tree: the presence of a happy family all wrapped up in each other.
–Burton Hillis

Christmas Comfort Foods

Kielbasa Bean Soup

Tara Black
Logan, UT

One night I wanted to make a hearty, spicy soup, so I just started tossing ingredients that sounded good together into my soup pot. I had a couple friends come over to sample it. They loved it and asked for my recipe, so I realized that I needed to write it down. We have a garden each year, and I love to add some of my homemade salsa to the soup. It gives it a boost of fresh flavor! Serve with croutons, or garlic bread for dipping.

1 lb. ground beef
1 lb. Kielbasa sausage,
　　thinly sliced
2 to 3 potatoes, peeled if desired
　　and diced
1 c. onion, diced
1 c. green pepper, diced
1 c. carrots, peeled and
　　shredded carrots
1 T. garlic, chopped

1-oz. pkg. beefy onion soup mix
2 14-1/2 oz. cans stewed
　　tomatoes, diced, or
　　4 c. favorite salsa
2 c. tomato juice
2 16-oz. cans Great Northern
　　beans, drained
16-oz. can pinto beans, drained
salt and pepper to taste

Brown beef and sausage together in a large soup pot over medium heat; drain. Add vegetables and garlic; sauté for 10 to 15 minutes, until lightly golden and partially tender. Sprinkle soup mix over mixture and stir in. Add undrained tomatoes or salsa, tomato juice, beans and seasonings. Bring to a gentle boil, stirring occasionally. Cook for 35 to 45 minutes, until potatoes are tender. Makes 8 to 10 servings.

Fill an apothecary jar with old-fashioned ribbon candy...
so pretty to look at and sweet to enjoy!

Comfort in a Soup Bowl

Beer Cheese Soup

*Shari Schiltz
New Ulm, MN*

*My family & friends just love this soup! It's great
on cold winter nights.*

1/2 lb. bacon, cut into
   1/3-inch pieces
1/2 c. onion, finely chopped
1 green pepper, finely chopped
1/4 c. butter, sliced
1/4 c. all-purpose flour
2 c. chicken broth
1 c. whipping cream

1-1/2 c. regular or non-alcoholic
   beer
1-1/2 c. shredded sharp
   Cheddar cheese
1/2 c. shredded Pepper
   Jack cheese
salt and pepper to taste

Cook bacon in a skillet over medium heat for 7 minutes, or until crisp.
Drain, reserving 1-1/2 tablespoons drippings in pan. Add onion and
green pepper to skillet; cook for 5 minutes. Reduce heat to medium-low.
Add butter and stir until melted; sprinkle with flour. Cook and stir until
slightly thickened. Stir in remaining ingredients. Simmer over low heat
for about 25 minutes, stirring occasionally. Makes 6 to 8 servings.

Do you have a grapevine wreath that's become a bit tattered? Spray
paint it all white, then sprinkle with fine white glitter for icy sparkle.
The textures will pop out and a whole new wreath will emerge.

Christmas
Comfort Foods

Chicken Tortilla Soup

Lori Simmons
Princeville, IL

This slow-cooker recipe won first place in a soup contest!
If you don't care for black beans, swap them out for red or
white beans. This recipe is great for a low-carb diet.

3 14-1/2 oz. cans chicken broth
2 10-oz. cans diced tomatoes
    with green chiles
2 15-1/2 oz. cans black beans
1 c. favorite salsa
1-oz. pkg. taco seasoning mix

1-oz. pkg. ranch salad dressing
    mix
4 boneless, skinless chicken
    breasts
Garnish: tortilla chips, shredded
    Mexican-blend cheese

In a 6-quart slow cooker, combine chicken broth, tomatoes with juice, beans, salsa and seasoning mixes; stir well. Add chicken; push down into broth mixture. Cover and cook on low setting for 6 to 8 hours, until chicken is very tender. Shred chicken in slow cooker, using 2 forks; mix well. Serve topped with tortilla chips and cheese. Makes 6 to 8 servings.

Soup suppers are a fuss-free way to get together with friends, neighbors and extended family. Set up a buffet table, decorate simply with holly and greenery and it's all set. Each family brings a favorite soup to share, along with copies of the recipe. What a delicious way to celebrate the season and maybe find a new favorite!

Comfort in a
Soup Bowl

Stuffed Pepper Soup

Audrey Szostak
Elmira, NY

An old favorite, ready to serve in a jiffy!

8.8-oz. pkg. ready-cook rice,
  uncooked
1 lb. ground beef
1 c. frozen chopped onion
2 c. frozen chopped green pepper

26-oz. jar chunky tomato
  pasta sauce
14-1/2 oz. can Italian-seasoned
  diced tomatoes
14-oz. can beef broth

Prepare rice according to package directions; set aside. Meanwhile, in a large saucepan over medium heat, brown beef with onion and green pepper; drain. Stir in pasta sauce, tomatoes with juice, beef broth and cooked rice; heat through. Makes 6 to 8 servings.

Chicken Cheese Soup

Alice Joy Randall
Nacogdoches, TX

This slow-cooker soup is wonderful for feeding a crowd. If you prefer a thinner soup, stir in 1/2 cup of water.

16-oz. pkg. Mexican pasteurized
  process cheese, cubed
3 10-oz. cans diced tomatoes
  with green chiles
2 12-oz. cans chicken

3 10-3/4 oz. cans cream of
  chicken soup
3 16-oz. cans Great Northern
  beans, drained
2 14-3/4 oz. cans creamed corn

In a microwave-safe dish, melt cheese with tomatoes in the microwave; stir well. Transfer cheese mixture to a 5-quart slow cooker; stir in remaining ingredients. Cover and cook on high setting for about one hour, until hot and bubbly. Makes 8 to 10 servings.

Keep jars of chicken and beef
bouillon cubes on hand for perking
up the flavor of a pot of soup.

Christmas
Comfort Foods

Easy Beef Barley Soup

Tamela James
Grove City, OH

This soup is absolutely delicious! I love recipes like this where you can basically just toss everything in the pot and let the magic work.

1 onion, chopped
1 clove garlic, minced
1 T. olive oil
14-1/2 oz. can diced tomatoes
6 c. beef broth
2 c. cooked roast beef, diced
2 carrots, peeled and sliced
1 stalk celery, sliced
1 c. sliced mushrooms

1/2 green pepper, diced
2/3 c. pearled barley, uncooked
1-oz. pkg. beef gravy mix
2 T. dried parsley
1 T. Worcestershire sauce
1/4 t. dried thyme
1 bay leaf
salt and pepper to taste

In a large soup pot over medium heat, cook onion and garlic in oil until soft. Add tomatoes with juice and remaining ingredients; bring to a boil. Reduce heat to medium-low. Simmer for 40 to 50 minutes, stirring occasionally, until barley is cooked. Remove bay leaf and serve. Makes 10 servings.

Start a family collection of ornaments for the Christmas tree! Try a theme like snowmen, reindeer, Santas or angels. Family members can add to it year 'round.

Comfort in a Soup Bowl

Irish Soda Bread

Laurie Malone
Wheeling, IL

In the 1940s, my paternal grandmother baked and sold Irish Soda Bread near a train station in Chicago. My mother baked it for my dad for Thanksgiving, Christmas, Saint Patrick's Day and Easter. It's wonderful with soup, or at just about any meal. I can still see Dad dipping it into his egg yolk on Christmas morning!

2-1/2 c. all-purpose flour
1/2 c. sugar
1-1/2 t. baking powder
1/2 t. baking soda
1/4 t. salt

1/4 c. butter, softened
1-1/4 c. raisins
1-1/4 c. buttermilk
1 egg, beaten

In a large bowl, mix flour, sugar, baking powder, baking soda and salt. With a fork or 2 knives, cut in butter to a cornmeal consistency. Fold in raisins. Add buttermilk and egg; stir until moistened. Pour batter into a greased 9"x5" loaf pan. Bake at 350 degrees for 60 to 65 minutes. Makes one loaf.

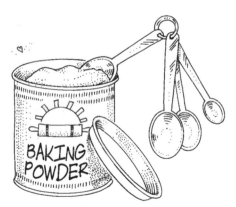

Not sure if that can of baking powder in the pantry is still good? Try this simple test: stir one teaspoon baking powder into 1/2 cup hot water. If it fizzes, go ahead and use it...if not, toss it out.

Christmas Comfort Foods

Snays' Southwest Chili

Mitchell Snay
Columbus, OH

After traveling to New Mexico, we started experimenting with Hatch chili powder. This recipe has become a favorite!

1 lb. ground beef
1/2 c. onion, diced
1-1/2 t. oil
14-1/2 oz. can diced tomatoes
1/2 c. water
1 T. New Mexican Hatch red
   chili powder

1 T. chili powder
1 t. ground cumin
1/8 t. cinnamon
1/8 t. cayenne pepper
15-1/2 oz. can light red kidney
   beans, drained

In a stockpot over medium heat, brown beef with onion in oil; drain. Add tomatoes with juice and remaining ingredients except beans; stir and bring to a boil. Reduce heat to medium-low. Simmer, uncovered, for 40 minutes, stirring occasionally. Add beans; cook over low heat for 20 minutes and serve. Makes 2 to 4 servings.

If your family gift list keeps growing, maybe it's time for a unique gift swap. Have each person draw a single name and spend a set amount like $10 on gifts that begin with the recipient's initial. For example, Barbara gets a book, bath beads or a bracelet. Be sure to open gifts at a family get-together...what fun!

Best Holiday
Sides &
Salads

Christmas Comfort Foods

Christmas Eve Salad

Lynnette Jones
East Flat Rock, NC

Our family always has pizza on Christmas Eve. Now that our children are grown and we have grandchildren, we have added a salad to the menu. This one is by far our favorite. The green salad with red cranberries is very festive. You can make your own candied pecans or use purchased ones.

12 to 16-oz. pkg. salad greens
2 red pears, peeled, cored
   and diced
6-oz. pkg. crumbled Gorgonzola
   cheese
1/2 c. dried cranberries
1/2 c. candied or toasted pecans,
   chopped

Combine all ingredients in a salad bowl; toss to mix. Pour desired amount of Dressing on salad. Toss to mix and serve. Makes 6 to 8 servings.

Dressing:

1/4 c. olive oil
1 T. Dijon mustard
1 T. pure maple syrup
1 t. cider vinegar

Combine all ingredients in a jar; add lid and shake well.

It's fun to hang little unexpected surprises from the dining room chandelier. Start with a swag of greenery, then tuck in Christmas whimsies like glass balls, tiny snowmen, cookie cutters and smiling Santas.

Sweet Potato Casserole

Tamela James
Grove City, OH

This was my dad's favorite sweet potato recipe. He said this was his meal and dessert all in one. My husband brought me the recipe from an office potluck, over 30 years ago. He doesn't like sweet potatoes himself, but knew I would love this recipe. I have made tweaks and changes over the years to suit our tastes.

29-oz. can cut sweet potatoes
1 c. butter, very well softened
1 c. all-purpose flour
1 c. brown sugar, packed

1 c. chopped pecans
1 c. flaked coconut
1 t. cinnamon

Spread undrained sweet potatoes in a lightly greased 13"x9" baking pan. Mash potatoes with a fork or a potato masher to desired consistency, leaving some lumps; do not mash until smooth. In a bowl, combine remaining ingredients; mix until crumbly and sprinkle over potatoes. Bake, uncovered, at 350 degrees for 45 minutes, or until hot and bubbly. Serves 10.

Vintage aprons are practical, and also adorable! Look for the 1950s style with poinsettias, snowmen and Santa Claus... perfect gifts for girlfriends who love to cook.

Christmas Comfort Foods

Green Bean Casserole

Charma Harrison
Piperton, TN

My mother-in-law made this casserole for special occasions. It's really delicious and just so different. I've discovered a few shortcuts that make it quick to prepare. The longer it's in the fridge, the better it tastes, and as the beans are eaten, you can add more drained cans of beans to the liquid and stretch it to make more meals.

3 to 4 14-1/2 oz. cans cut
  green beans
6 slices bacon, crisply cooked
  and crumbled, or 2.8-oz. pkg.
  real bacon bits
1 onion, chopped, or 1 T. dried,
  chopped onions

1/2 to 1 c. catsup, to taste
1 T. sugar or sugar substitute
1 T. Worcestershire sauce, or
  more to taste
1 t. red pepper flakes
salt and pepper to taste

Combine undrained beans and remaining ingredients in a lightly greased 3-quart casserole dish. Bake, uncovered, at 325 degrees for 30 to 40 minutes, or microwave on high for 10 to 15 minutes, until hot and bubbly. Best made early in the day or even the day before, as the longer it stands, the more flavor it develops. This dish reheats well. Makes 8 servings.

Saucy Bacon Asparagus

Nancy Wise
Little Rock, AR

An easy way to make fresh asparagus special.

1-1/2 lbs. fresh asparagus
  spears, trimmed
1 T. water

3 slices bacon
1/2 c. onion, chopped
1/2 c. ranch salad dressing

Add asparagus and water to a microwave-safe dish; partially cover with plastic wrap. Microwave on high for 4 to 5 minutes, until crisp-tender. Meanwhile, cook bacon in a skillet until crisp. Drain bacon on paper towels. Drain drippings from skillet, but do not rinse skillet. Add onion to skillet; cook and stir until tender. Stir in salad dressing. Drain asparagus; top with sauce and crumbled bacon. Serves 6.

Not Your Usual Broccoli Casserole

Ruth Rinker
Valparaiso, IN

I got this recipe in the mid-70s and have made it dozens of times. It's understood by everyone that this dish will show up at any and every family gathering! I use some shortcuts, like cheese crumbles instead of dicing from a block. And, I mix it all in the pan it's going to be baked in...one less bowl to wash!

24-oz. container small-curd
   cottage cheese
6 eggs
6 T. all-purpose flour
20-oz. pkg. frozen chopped
   broccoli crowns

8-oz. pkg. pasteurized process
   cheese crumbles
6 T. butter, melted
paprika to taste

Spread cottage cheese in a greased 13"x9" baking pan; set aside. In the empty cottage cheese container, whisk together eggs and flour; add to cottage cheese in pan and mix. Stir in frozen broccoli and cheese crumbles until blended. Smooth top of mixture with spoon as much as possible. Drizzle evenly with melted butter; sprinkle with paprika. Bake, uncovered, at 350 degrees for about 40 minutes, until set but not dry. Serves 10 to 12.

A friend who bakes would love to receive a cookbook tucked in the pocket of a potholder. Remember to tuck in recipe cards sharing some family favorites, too!

Christmas Comfort Foods

Winter Garden Salad

Karen Wilson
Defiance, OH

*This is a delicious, easy make-ahead salad. Perfect for
the busy holiday days!*

1 head cauliflower, cut into
    bite-size pieces
1 bunch broccoli, cut into
    bite-size pieces
1/2 c. onion, chopped
1/4 c. green onions, chopped

1/4 c. celery, chopped
1/2 c. carrot, peeled and chopped
1 c. Cheddar cheese, diced
1/4 c. bacon, crisply cooked
    and crumbled

Combine all ingredients in a salad bowl; toss to mix. Pour Dressing over
all; toss again. Cover and refrigerate for 8 to 10 hours. Toss again just
before serving. Makes 8 servings.

Dressing:

1/2 c. mayonnaise
1/3 c. vinegar

1/3 c. oil
1/3 c. sugar

Combine all ingredients in a jar; add lid and shake well.

Enjoy some old-fashioned family fun, stringing popcorn and
cranberries together. The kids will love it, and the strands are
so pretty draped along a mantel, doorway and, of course,
on the Christmas tree!

Best Holiday
Sides & Salads

Aunt Marge's Deluxe Corn Custard

Becky Myers
Ashland, OH

My Aunt Marge always brought this dish to our family gatherings. It's the creamiest, dreamiest vegetable you will ever eat! This is true comfort in a casserole dish. If you double the recipe, bake it just a little longer.

3 T. butter, melted
3 T. cornstarch
2 eggs, beaten
1 c. milk

1/4 c. sugar
1/4 t. salt
15-1/4 oz. can creamed corn
10-oz. pkg. frozen corn

In a large bowl, stir together melted butter and cornstarch. Add remaining ingredients; mix well. Spoon into a greased 2-quart casserole dish. Bake, uncovered, at 350 degrees for one hour, or until bubbly and golden. Serves 6.

When you have family members visiting for the holidays, especially those who live far away, get out the old picture albums, slides and family movies. What a joy to reminisce together, laugh and share special memories of childhood and Christmases past!

Christmas Comfort Foods

Sheet Pan Squash & Kale Salad

Linda Nielsen
British Columbia, Canada

*A very tasty salad! This recipe is a great one to take to potlucks.
I am always asked for the recipe by at least one person,
every time I serve it.*

4 c. butternut squash, peeled,
   seeded and cubed
1 T. cold-pressed canola oil or
   extra-virgin olive oil
1/2 t. cinnamon

1/2 t. pepper
6 c. fresh kale, thinly sliced
1 c. red onion, thinly sliced
1/2 c. dried cranberries
1/2 c. pumpkin seeds

In a large bowl, toss together squash and oil. Sprinkle with seasonings; toss well to coat. Spread squash evenly on a parchment paper-lined baking pan. Bake at 375 degrees for 30 minutes, or until soft. Remove from oven; let stand for 5 minutes. Meanwhile, in the same bowl, toss together remaining ingredients. Pour Dressing over salad; toss to coat. Add squash; gently toss again and serve. Makes 8 servings.

Dressing:

1 T. cold-pressed canola oil or
   extra-virgin olive oil
2 T. cider vinegar

2 t. pure maple syrup
1 t. Dijon mustard

In a small bowl, whisk together all ingredients.

A Christmas family party...we know of nothing in nature more delightful! There seems a magic in the very name of Christmas.
–Charles Dickens

Best Holiday
Sides & Salads

Midwestern Comfort Potatoes

Margo King
Woodstock, IL

My girls love these potatoes! Fixing this recipe makes the whole house smell good. It's an easy recipe to do overnight or in the early morning, so it's ready for dinner. I usually double the recipe in a larger slow cooker when taking to a large gathering.

32-oz. pkg. frozen diced
    hashbrown potatoes, thawed
Optional: 1/2 c. onion, chopped
10-3/4 oz. can cream of
    chicken soup
1 to 2 c. sour cream

1 t. salt
1 t. pepper
2 1/4 c. shredded Cheddar
    cheese
2 c. corn flake cereal, crushed
1/2 c. butter, melted

Spray a 5-quart slow cooker with non-stick vegetable spray; set aside. In a large bowl, combine all ingredients except corn flakes and butter; add to crock. Cover and cook on low setting for 6 hours, stirring occasionally, or until potatoes are soft and cooked through. Shortly before serving time, make topping. Toss corn flakes with melted butter; spread evenly on a parchment paper-lined baking sheet. Bake at 350 degrees for 15 minutes, or until lightly golden. Spoon corn flake mixture over potatoes in crock and serve. Makes 8 to 10 servings.

Food for friends doesn't have to be fancy...your guests will be delighted with comfort foods like Mom used to make. Invite them to help themselves from large platters set right on the table. So family-friendly, and a perfect time to use your holiday dishes.

Christmas
Comfort Foods

Christmas Peas

*Judy Lange
Imperial, PA*

*This recipe is a tasty change from the usual holiday green beans.
I usually make both dishes for Christmas dinner.*

2 10-oz. pkgs. frozen peas
2 10-3/4 oz. cans cream of
    mushroom soup
1/2 c. milk

1/2 t. salt
1/2 t. pepper
1 c. shredded Cheddar cheese
1 c. French fried onions, divided

In a large saucepan, cook frozen peas according to package directions;
drain. Add remaining ingredients, reserving half of onions for topping;
transfer to a greased 2-quart casserole dish. Bake, uncovered, at
350 degrees for 20 minutes. Remove from oven; top with reserved
onion rings. Bake for another 10 minutes, or until hot and bubbly.
Makes 10 servings.

Orange-Glazed Carrots

*Jen Thomas
Santa Rosa, CA*

Even my pickier kids love these sweet carrots!

1-1/2 lbs. baby carrots
2 T. butter
1/3 c. brown sugar, packed

1/2 t. salt
1/2 t. orange zest

In a large saucepan over medium heat, cover carrots with water; cook
for 15 minutes. Meanwhile, melt butter in a skillet; add remaining
ingredients and cook until bubbly. Drain carrots and add to skillet. Cook
over low heat stirring occasionally, until carrots are tender and glazed.
Makes 6 servings.

Wrap orange peels and store in the
freezer...ready to grate whenever
a recipe calls for fresh citrus zest.

Best Holiday
Sides & Salads

Creamed Onions

Shirl Parsons
Cape Carteret, NC

This is an old 1950s recipe my mom used to make.
It's still a favorite at holidays.

12 medium sweet onions, halved
3/4 c. butter, divided
1/4 c. all-purpose flour
2 c. milk

1 t. salt
grated Parmesan cheese and
  paprika to taste

In a large skillet over medium heat, sauté onions gently in 1/2 cup butter until tender; drain. Arrange onions cut-side down in a buttered 13"x9" shallow baking pan. Melt remaining butter in a saucepan over low heat; remove from heat and blend in flour. Gradually stir in milk; add salt. Cook over medium heat, stirring constantly until thickened. Pour over onions. Sprinkle generously with cheese; sprinkle with paprika. Bake, uncovered, at 350 degrees for 20 minutes. Serves 12.

Lemon–Roasted Brussels Sprouts

Ann Farris
Biscoe, AR

This is an easy, healthy recipe. On Christmas, it can be prepped ahead and then popped in the oven once the roast turkey is done.

1 lb. fresh Brussels sprouts,
  trimmed and halved
1 T. olive oil

juice of one lemon
garlic powder, salt and pepper
  to taste

Place Brussels sprouts in a plastic zipping bag; add remaining ingredients. Seal bag; toss to coat sprouts well and refrigerate overnight. Shortly before serving time, spread sprouts on a lightly greased baking sheet. Bake at 400 degrees for 15 to 20 minutes. Serves 6.

A quick cheese sauce for veggies!
Combine one cup evaporated milk and 1/2 cup shredded cheese.
Cook and stir over low heat until smooth.

Christmas
Comfort Foods

Ma's Turkey Stuffing

Barbara Bazel
Chicago, IL

Everyone who's ever tasted this stuffing says it's the best they've had...even a few people who don't like stuffing! My grandmother made this from the earliest time I can remember, then my mother took over and now I make it for my family.

2 lbs. ground pork sausage
2 onions, chopped
1 stalk celery, chopped
1/4 c. butter
2 loaves sliced bread, torn into
   little pieces

2 eggs, beaten
14-oz. can chicken broth
1 T. poultry seasoning
1/2 c. milk
salt and pepper to taste
Garnish: additional butter

Brown sausage in a large skillet over medium heat; drain. Meanwhile, in a large saucepan, cook onions and celery in butter until tender. In a very large bowl, combine sausage and onion mixture; add bread, eggs, chicken broth and poultry seasoning. With your hands, mix in just enough milk until mixture feels gooey. Spread mixture in a greased 13"x9" deep baking pan. Season with salt and pepper; dot with a few pats of butter. Cover with aluminum foil. Bake at 350 degrees for 1-1/2 to 2 hours, removing foil after one hour. Stuffing may also be baked in a turkey; add salt and pepper to mixture before stuffing turkey and bake as usual. Makes 8 to 10 servings.

Cut leftover bread into cubes, pack into freezer bags and freeze for making stuffing cubes. Whether you call it stuffing, dressing or even filling, it's best made with day-old bread, which keeps its texture better than very fresh bread.

Best Holiday
Sides & Salads

Broccoli Pasta Slaw

Carolyn Gochenaur
Howe, IN

One day, my sister and I saw this recipe on a TV cooking show. So we tried it and liked it a lot! Almonds and raisins make it festive for the holidays. I've been asked for the recipe several times.

8-oz. pkg. bowtie pasta,
　　uncooked
16-oz. pkg. broccoli slaw

1 c. slivered almonds
1 c. dark or golden raisins

Cook pasta according to package directions; drain. Rinse with cold water; drain again and place in a large bowl. Add slaw, almonds and raisins. Pour Dressing over pasta mixture; stir to coat. Serve immediately and refrigerate any leftovers. Serves 6.

Dressing:

1 c. low-fat plain yogurt
1/2 c. mayonnaise
6 T. cider vinegar

2 T. sugar
1/4 to 1/2 t. cayenne pepper
salt and pepper to taste

Whisk together all ingredients until sugar dissolves.

Mix up a yummy vinaigrette for salads in a nearly empty honey bottle. Add 1/4 cup oil, 2 tablespoons lemon juice and one tablespoon Dijon mustard to the bottle. Add the lid, shake well and squeeze, using the handy spout.

Christmas
Comfort Foods

Special Bing Cherry Salad

Judy Taylor
Butler, MO

I have been making this salad for a number of years. It is wonderful any time of year, and perfect for the holidays when you want that "special" salad. It complements the Thanksgiving turkey or the Christmas ham very well. It is a pretty salad in a clear bowl, and so good, you can almost call it dessert!

14-oz. can sweetened
    condensed milk
1/3 c. lemon juice
15-oz. can pitted dark sweet
    cherries, drained
20-oz. can pineapple tidbits,
    drained

16-oz. container frozen whipped
    topping, thawed
1/2 c. chopped pecans, or more
    to taste, divided

In a large bowl, whisk together condensed milk and lemon juice; cover and refrigerate for one hour. Add remaining ingredients, reserving a few pecans for garnish; mix well. Top with reserved pecans; cover and chill until serving time. Makes 6 to 8 servings.

It wouldn't be Christmas without Charles Dickens! Find a local production of " A Christmas Carol" and take everyone to see it. Whether it's a lavish stage production or a small amateur show, the story remains the same familiar treat every time.

Million-Dollar Frozen Cranberry Salad

Gladys & Edward Kielar
Whitehouse, OH

With this salad, any day can be a holiday…it's a real favorite in our family! It's delicious and so easy to make. I freeze bags of cranberries in the fall so I can make cranberry desserts all year long.

14-oz. can sweetened
   condensed milk
1/4 c. lemon juice
14-oz. can whole-berry
   cranberry sauce
15-1/4 oz. can crushed
   pineapple, drained

1/2 c. chopped walnuts
8-oz. container frozen whipped
   topping, thawed
Garnish: lettuce leaves,
   additional whipped topping
   and walnuts

In a large bowl, whisk together condensed milk and lemon juice. Stir in cranberry sauce, pineapple and walnuts. Fold in whipped topping. Spread in an ungreased 13"x9" glass baking pan. Cover and freeze until firm. Remove from freezer 10 minutes before serving. Cut into squares. Serve on lettuce leaves, garnished with whipped topping and a sprinkle of walnuts. Makes 16 servings.

Mix up a yummy topping for fruity gelatin salads. Beat 8 ounces softened cream cheese until fluffy. Fold in 8 ounces sour cream and 1/2 cup powdered sugar. Dollop onto gelatin salads and garnish with chopped nuts, if you wish.

Christmas Comfort Foods

Sweet Potato, Apple & Cranberry Bake

Suzanne Ramey
Allendale, MI

A scrumptious family favorite that I'm asked to make every holiday season.

6 sweet potatoes
2 c. fresh or frozen cranberries
1 c. water
1 c. sugar
1 apple, peeled, cored and
    thinly sliced

1/2 c. light brown sugar, packed
1/4 t. cinnamon
1/4 c. butter, melted
1/2 c. orange juice
6-oz. pkg. pecan halves

Place sweet potatoes in a large saucepan; add enough water to cover potatoes. Bring to a boil over high heat; cover and cook until potatoes are fork-tender. Drain; cool slightly. Peel and slice potatoes. Meanwhile, in another saucepan, combine cranberries, water and sugar. Cook over medium heat for about 15 minutes, until cranberries pop; drain. In a greased 13"x9" baking pan, layer sweet potatoes, apple slices and cranberries. Sprinkle with brown sugar and cinnamon; drizzle with melted butter and orange juice. Arrange pecan halves on top. Bake, uncovered, at 350 degrees for 30 minutes, or until bubbly and potatoes are tender. Makes 6 to 8 servings.

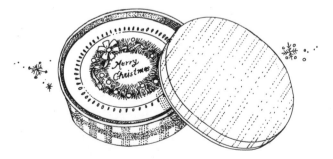

Don't save them for "someday," make some memories now...
go ahead and use Grandma's best china and silver!

Best Holiday
Sides & Salads

Ranch Potato Casserole

Sandra Turner
Fayetteville, NC

*This is an easy side dish that can be served with a variety
of main dishes. I really enjoy it with baked ham.*

6 to 8 potatoes, peeled
   and quartered
1/4 c. bacon, crisply cooked
   and crumbled
1/2 c. sour cream

1/2 c. ranch salad dressing
2 T. fresh parsley, chopped
1-1/2 c. shredded Cheddar
   cheese, divided

In a large saucepan, cover potatoes with water. Cook over high heat
until potatoes are fork-tender; drain. Transfer potatoes to a greased
13"x9" baking pan; set aside. In a bowl, combine remaining ingredients,
reserving 1/2 cup cheese for topping. Spoon mixture over potatoes and
toss gently; top with reserved cheese. Bake, uncovered, at 350 degrees
for 40 to 45 minutes. Serves 6 to 8.

Creamy Mashed Potatoes

Tiffany Jones
Batesville, AR

*My husband Andy and son Noah absolutely love my mashed potatoes.
For Noah's special birthday dinner, he even requested Mommy's
mashed potatoes. Your family will love them too! I don't add salt,
because my mom is on a low-sodium diet and the bouillon cubes give
it plenty of flavor.*

5 lbs. Yukon Gold potatoes,
   peeled and cubed
6 cubes chicken bouillon

3 T. butter
2 T. milk
pepper to taste

Place potatoes and bouillon cubes in a stockpot; cover completely with
water. Boil over high heat for about 15 minutes, until potatoes are
fork-tender; drain. Add butter; beat with an electric mixer on medium
speed. Slowly add milk, beating until creamy. Season with pepper as
desired. Makes 6 servings.

Christmas
Comfort Foods

English Pea Casserole

Kathy Barry
Bonaire, GA

This is a family favorite, and is also highly requested for luncheons at work. Sometimes I don't make it to the sign-up sheet fast enough... but somebody has already written down my name for this recipe! Easy to make, and a perfect side dish for all occasions.

3 to 4 15-oz. cans young sweet
    peas, drained
10-3/4 oz. can cream of
    mushroom soup
8-oz. container sour cream

1 t. garlic powder
1 c. shredded Cheddar cheese
1-1/2 sleeves round buttery
    crackers, crushed
3/4 c. margarine, melted

Add peas to a bowl; set aside. In another bowl, mix mushroom soup, sour cream and garlic powder. Fold into peas; transfer to a lightly greased 3-quart casserole dish. Top with shredded cheese and crushed crackers. Drizzle melted margarine over crackers. Bake, uncovered, at 350 degrees for 45 minutes to one hour, until hot and bubbly. Makes 6 to 8 servings.

As Christmas nears, plan a family slumber party! Set up quilts and sleeping bags around the tree, pass around lots of snacks and watch a holiday movie. Before falling asleep, read "The Night Before Christmas" with only the tree lights on.

Mom's Cheesy Broccoli Bake

Sue Klapper
Muskego, WI

*My mother always served this dish for special family dinners,
and I've continued the tradition. It's real comfort food for
my guests and me. Enjoy!*

10-oz. frozen chopped broccoli
10-3/4 oz. can cream of
    mushroom soup
1/2 c. shredded Cheddar cheese
1 egg, beaten

1/4 c. mayonnaise
1/4 c. milk
1 T. butter, melted
1/4 c. dry bread crumbs

Cook broccoli according to package directions; drain. Meanwhile, in a
large bowl, blend mushroom soup, cheese and egg; stir in mayonnaise
and milk. Fold in broccoli; transfer to a lightly greased 10"x6" baking
pan. In a small bowl, mix melted butter and bread crumbs; sprinkle on
top. Bake, uncovered, at 375 degrees for 30 to 35 minutes, until bubbly
and crumbs are golden. Makes 6 servings.

Make mini wreaths of rosemary to slip around dinner napkins.
Simply wind fresh rosemary stems into a ring shape, tuck in
the ends and tie on a tiny bow...so festive!

Christmas Comfort Foods

Kathy's Sage Dressing

*Kathy Courington
Canton, GA*

I made this dressing for a Christmas party and was a little apprehensive, as I had never made dressing in a slow cooker before. I needn't have worried...everyone loved it! There was only a spoonful left.

1 onion, chopped
1/2 c. celery, chopped
6 T. butter, divided
12-oz. pkg. cornbread stuffing
12-oz. pkg. herb-seasoned
   stuffing
4 eggs, lightly beaten

2 T. dried sage
1 t. salt
1/2 t. pepper
2 10-3/4 oz. cans cream of
   chicken soup
2 to 4 14-oz. cans chicken broth

In a skillet over medium heat, sauté onion and celery in 2 tablespoons butter for about 5 minutes. In a large bowl, combine cornbread stuffing, seasoned stuffing, onion mixture, eggs, seasonings and soup; mix well. Add 2 cans broth and mix well. Additional broth may be added, depending on moistness desired. Spoon into a greased 6-quart slow cooker; dot with remaining butter. Cover and cook on high setting for 2 hours, or on low setting for 4 hours. If mixture becomes too dry, add more broth or water. Serves 12 to 16.

Write out the menu for a special holiday meal and place in an elegant frame...dinner guests will be looking forward to each delicious dish!

Best Holiday
Sides & Salads

Sautéed Green Beans & Mushrooms

Julia Bondi
Chicago, IL

This recipe is fresh-tasting, quick and delicious.

1 lb. fresh green beans, trimmed
    and sliced
3 T. onion, chopped
1 to 2 T. garlic, chopped
6 T. butter

4-oz. can sliced mushrooms,
    drained
2 T. plus 1 t. brown sugar,
    packed

Fill a skillet half-full of water; bring to a boil over high heat. Add green beans and cook until crisp-tender. Drain and set aside. In the same skillet over medium heat, sauté onion and garlic in butter until translucent. Return beans to skillet; add mushrooms and sauté until very lightly golden. Add brown sugar; stir until dissolved and serve. Makes 6 to 8 servings.

Cheesy Cauliflower Dish

Irene Robinson
Cincinnati, OH

Creamy, quick and oh-so easy...a great way to jazz up cauliflower!

1 small head cauliflower, cut into
    bite-size flowerets
1/2 c. shredded Cheddar cheese

10-3/4 oz. can cream of
    celery soup

Add cauliflower to a saucepan of boiling water. Cook over medium-high heat for 15 to 20 minutes, until tender. Drain; place in a greased 9"x9" baking pan. Combine cheese and soup in a bowl; spoon over cauliflower. Bake, uncovered, at 350 degrees for 15 to 20 minutes, until hot and bubbly. Makes 6 servings.

A dollop of lemon butter adds flavor to steamed vegetables. Simply blend 2 tablespoons softened butter with the zest of one lemon.

Christmas
Comfort Foods

Maple Baked Beans With Apples

Bev Traxler
British Columbia, Canada

This recipe for baked beans has so many good flavors in it...we all love it! For crowd-size entertaining, double the recipe, using one package each of black-eyed peas and white pea beans.

1 lb. pkg. dried black-eyed peas
   or white pea beans, rinsed
   and sorted
6 c. water
1 c. onion, chopped
1/4 lb. salt pork or bacon, cut
   into 1/2-inch pieces
1/2 c. pure maple syrup
1/3 c. chili sauce

2 T. molasses
2 t. Dijon mustard
2 t. salt
3 Granny Smith apples, cored
   and cut into 8 slices each
1/3 c. brown sugar, packed
1/4 c. butter, melted
Optional: 1/4 c. rum

Place peas or beans in a large saucepan; add water and let stand overnight. In the morning, do not drain; bring beans and soaking water to a boil over high heat. Reduce heat to medium-low; cover and simmer for one hour, or until tender. Drain, reserving cooking liquid. In a greased 2-quart casserole dish, combine beans, onion, salt pork or bacon, maple syrup, chili sauce, molasses, mustard and salt. Add enough of reserved cooking liquid to cover beans; stir well. Cover and bake at 350 degrees for 3 hours, stirring occasionally and adding more liquid as needed to keep beans barely covered. Uncover; arrange apple slices on top. Sprinkle with brown sugar and drizzle with melted butter. Bake for one hour longer, or until apples are tender. Just before serving, drizzle with rum, if using. Makes 8 servings.

Don't have a fireplace mantel for hanging stockings? Fasten Shaker pegs to a wooden board, one for each member of the family.

Toffee Apple Salad

Joan Baker
Westland, MI

My aunt gave this recipe to my mom 25 years ago, and it has been a favorite of family & friends ever since. If there isn't enough pineapple juice to cover the apples, add a little lemon-lime soda.

4 Gala, Fuji or Honey Crisp
   apples, cored and cubed
4 Granny Smith apples, cored
   and cubed
20-oz. can crushed pineapple,
   drained and juice reserved
2 pasteurized eggs, beaten

1 c. sugar
2 T. all-purpose flour
2 T. cider vinegar
8-oz. container frozen whipped
   topping, thawed
16-oz. jar unsalted roasted
   peanuts, chopped and divided

In a large bowl, combine apples and reserved pineapple juice. Mix gently and set aside. In another large bowl, combine eggs, sugar, flour and vinegar; beat well. Fold in whipped topping, pineapple and peanuts, reserving 1/4 cup peanuts for topping. Drain apples and stir into pineapple mixture. Sprinkle reserved peanuts on top. Cover and chill. For the best consistency, make and serve the same day. Makes 8 to 10 servings.

String an assortment of ribbon candy onto a holiday wreath and attach a small scissors on a ribbon. Family & friends will love to snip off a treat!

Christmas
Comfort Foods

Spinach–Cheese Squares

Earline Monahan
Hyde Park, VT

So good...perfect for a serve-yourself holiday buffet.

1 c. all-purpose flour
1 t. baking powder
3 eggs, beaten
1 c. milk
1/4 c. butter, melted
1 T. green onions, chopped

salt to taste
2 10-oz. pkgs. frozen chopped
   spinach, thawed and well
   drained
16-oz. pkg. shredded Cheddar
   cheese

In a large bowl, combine all ingredients except spinach and cheese; mix well. Fold in spinach and cheese. Spread evenly in a lightly greased 13"x9" baking pan. Bake, uncovered, at 350 degrees for 35 to 40 minutes, until set and cheese is melted. Cut into squares to serve. Makes 8 to 10 servings.

Roast Asparagus

Marian Forck
Chamois, MO

My girlfriend shared this recipe with me. We used to work together and shared our garden vegetables and recipes.

3 T. olive oil, divided
1 to 2 lbs. fresh asparagus,
   trimmed
2 t. garlic powder

2 t. seasoned salt
1 t. pepper
Optional: grated Parmesan
   cheese

Spread one tablespoon oil in a jelly-roll pan. Arrange asparagus in single layer in pan; drizzle with remaining oil. Shake pan to coat asparagus with oil; sprinkle with seasonings. Bake at 450 degrees, thin spears 5 to 7 minutes, medium spears 7 to 10 minutes, thick spears 9 to 11 minutes. If desired, sprinkle with Parmesan cheese before serving. Serves 6.

Try barley pilaf for a change from rice. Prepare quick-cooking barley with chicken broth instead of water. Season with a little chopped onion and dried parsley. Quick and tasty!

Best Holiday
Sides & Salads

Steph's Tortellini Salad

Stephanie Heisey
Manheim, PA

My daughter Heather and I make this salad for all our family get-togethers. It's festive, easy to toss together and a great make-ahead, as it can be prepared the day before.

16-oz. pkg. refrigerated cheese
    tortellini, uncooked
12-oz. jar marinated artichokes,
    drained and chopped
7-oz. jar roasted red peppers,
    drained and chopped

1/4 lb. pepperoni, chopped
12-oz. pkg. shredded Italian-
    blend cheese
16-oz. bottle Italian salad
    dressing

Cook tortellini according to package directions, just until tender. Drain and put in a large bowl. Add artichokes, red peppers and pepperoni; sprinkle with cheese. Add desired amount of salad dressing and stir thoroughly. Cover and chill until serving time, occasionally adding a little more dressing as needed. Makes 10 servings.

Dollar stores can be gold mines for fun stocking stuffers. Year 'round, watch for tiny games and puzzles, wind-up toys, mini bath products and even bite-size treats...keep your finds in a big well-hidden box. On Christmas Eve, you'll have plenty of surprises to tuck into stockings!

Christmas Comfort Foods

Jackie's Macaroni & Cheese

Leslie Harvie
Simpsonville, SC

This easy slow-cooker recipe has been in my family for years. My Great-Aunt Jackie gave it to my newlywed mother in the 1970s, and it is still a must-have dish at every family gathering.

16-oz. pkg. elbow macaroni,
  uncooked
1/2 c. butter, melted
Optional: salt and pepper to taste
10-3/4 oz. can Cheddar cheese
  soup

12-oz. can evaporated milk
2 eggs
3/4 c. whole milk
16-oz. pkg. shredded sharp
  Cheddar cheese, divided
Garnish: paprika

Cook macaroni according to package directions, just until tender; drain. Drizzle with butter; season with salt and pepper, if desired. Transfer cooked macaroni to a 6-quart slow cooker; set aside. In a bowl, whisk together cheese soup and evaporated milk; set aside. In another bowl, beat eggs; whisk in whole milk. To macaroni in slow cooker, add soup mixture, egg mixture and cheese, reserving 1/2 cup cheese for topping. Sprinkle with remaining cheese and paprika. Cover and cook on low setting for 3 hours, or until hot and bubbly. Serves 8.

Have you ever sampled Sugar-on-Snow? Gather a pail of freshly fallen snow, spoon it into serving bowls and top with warm maple syrup. A wonderful New England wintertime treat!

Best Holiday
Sides & Salads

Holiday Broccoli Salad

Sandy Ward
Anderson, IN

Mom always made a feast for us at Thanksgiving and Christmas. That meant plenty of food, which included several different salads...all of them made with love, all of them great. This is a wonderful salad to serve with wraps, burgers and hot dogs, and at Christmas it makes a festive side, so pretty. Hope your holidays will build lasting memories of love, family & friends!

2 bunches broccoli, cut into
    small flowerets
8 slices bacon, crisply cooked
    and crumbled
1/2 red onion, diced

1/2 c. golden raisins
1 c. mayonnaise
1/2 c. sugar
2 t. vinegar

In a large bowl, combine broccoli, bacon, onion and raisins, toss to mix and set aside. In another bowl, combine mayonnaise, sugar and vinegar; mix well and spoon over broccoli mixture. Toss together; serve immediately, or cover and chill. Makes 8 servings.

A length of wire makes it easy to secure evergreen branches to a mailbox. Use chenille stems to wire on berry bunches and a bow, then tuck in a surprise for the letter carrier!

Christmas
Comfort Foods

Christmas Cinnamon Apples

Jill Ball
Highland, UT

This is a beautiful dish to serve for Christmas and special occasions. It is beautiful, yummy and easy to make... always a must for holidays!

9 Golden Delicious apples, peeled
3 c. water
3 c. sugar
1 t. cinnamon

several drops red food coloring
1/4 c. chopped dates
2 T. chopped almonds
Garnish: whipped cream

Core apples, but do not cut through the bottom; set aside. In a large stockpot over medium-high heat, bring water, sugar and cinnamon to a boil. Add apples and desired amount of food coloring; cooked apples will darken as they cool. Bring to a boil; simmer until apples are tender. Remove apples to a large bowl; let cool. In a small bowl, mix dates and almonds. Spoon mixture into apples; top with whipped cream and serve. Makes 9 servings.

Hats, mittens and woolly scarves can be picked up for almost nothing at summer yard sales, so fill a "snowman" box to keep in the garage. Kids can grab a carrot "nose" from the fridge on the way outside... all set for that snow-day snowman. No more snowy boots in the house, looking for the essentials!

Best Holiday
Sides & Salads

Mother's Pickled Peaches

Margaret Welder
Madrid, IA

These peaches are wonderful served on a bed of lettuce with a scoop of cottage cheese. My mother always made this old-fashioned recipe for the holidays. It was a favorite of mine and of our family.

2 29-oz. cans peach halves in
  heavy syrup, drained and
  syrup reserved
1 c. cider vinegar

2 4-inch cinnamon sticks
1 T. whole cloves
1-1/2 to 3 c. sugar

In a large saucepan, combine reserved peach syrup, vinegar, cinnamon sticks, cloves and 1-1/2 cups sugar. (Use 3 cups sugar if peaches are canned in juice or light syrup.) Bring to a boil over high heat; cook and stir until sugar dissolves. Add peach halves and return to a boil. Remove from heat; cool at room temperature. Cover and refrigerate. To serve, remove peach halves from syrup with a slotted spoon. Serves 8 to 10.

Pomegranate-Apple Salad

Marie Smulski
Lyons, IL

You get tart and sweet in this refreshing salad. The pomegranate seeds look like little jewels and the pecans add crunch.

2 c. whipping cream
1/4 c. sugar
2 t. vanilla extract
1 Gala apple, peeled, cored
  and cubed

1 Golden Delicious apple, peeled,
  cored and cubed
2-1/2 c. pomegranate seeds
1 c. chopped pecans, toasted

In a chilled large glass bowl, beat cream with an electric mixer on high speed until soft peaks form. Add sugar and vanilla; beat until stiff peaks form. Fold in apples and pomegranate seeds; sprinkle with pecans. Serve immediately. Makes 8 servings.

For a quick & easy mantel decoration, spell out "Merry Christmas" with vintage alphabet blocks.

Christmas
Comfort Foods

Holiday Kraut

Barbara Hightower
Broomfield, CO

Sauerkraut with Christmas dinner? Yes, please! This recipe is delicious, especially with roast turkey, chicken and pork. My mother first tried it in the 1950s for our Christmas dinner after finding the recipe in a magazine. Our whole family has included it ever since as a main part of our Thanksgiving and Christmas dinners. Give it a try...you'll be surprised by how delicious it is!

32-oz. can sauerkraut, drained
   and rinsed
28-oz. can diced tomatoes

2 c. celery, chopped
1 c. brown sugar, packed,
1 to 2 T. butter, sliced

Preheat oven to 400 degrees. In a bowl, combine sauerkraut, tomatoes with juice, celery and brown sugar. Spoon into a greased 2-quart casserole dish; dot with butter. Cover dish and place in oven; immediately reduce oven to 300 degrees. Bake for 2 hours, or until sauerkraut is tender and a rich golden color. If becoming too dry, add a little water; if too juicy, uncover. Serves 10.

Ukrainian Sauerkraut & Beans

Ange Sukala
Williamsburg, PA

We've had this dish forever for Christmas Eve dinner at my parents' house! I'm passing the recipe on to my kids.

16-oz. jar sauerkraut, drained
2 14-1/2 oz. cans butter beans,
   drained and rinsed

2 T. catsup
salt and pepper to taste
1 T. butter

To a stockpot, add sauerkraut, beans, catsup and enough water to cover it all. Bring to a boil over high heat; reduce heat to medium-low. Simmer for 30 minutes, stirring occasionally. Season with salt and pepper; stir in butter just before serving. Makes 8 servings.

Potato Pierogi Casserole

Leona Krivda
Belle Vernon, PA

This dish is always good with the pork and sauerkraut on New Year's...a favorite at our house.

16-oz. pkg. lasagna noodles, uncooked
10 to 12 potatoes, peeled and quartered
1 to 2 t. salt
16-oz. pkg. shredded Cheddar cheese
3 onions, finely minced
1-1/4 c. butter
salt and pepper to taste

Cook noodles according to package directions; drain. Meanwhile, in a separate pan, cover potatoes with water; add salt. Bring to a boil over high heat; cook until potatoes are tender. Drain; add potatoes to a large bowl and mash. Add cheese; beat well and set aside. In a skillet over medium heat, sauté onions in butter until tender. Add 1/3 of onion mixture to potato mixture; season with salt and pepper. In a greased 13"x9" baking pan, layer 1/4 of cooked noodles to cover bottom of pan; cover with 1/3 of potato mixture. Repeat layering twice; end with noodles. Spread remaining onion mixture over the top. Cover with aluminum foil. Bake at 350 degrees for 30 minutes, or until heated through. Makes 8 servings.

Be sure to share family stories behind the special dishes that are a tradition at every holiday dinner. There may even be stories to tell about your vintage tablecloth or the whimsical salt & pepper shakers!

Christmas Comfort Foods

Sweet-and-Sour Bacon Cabbage

Mel Chencharick
Julian, PA

If you like cabbage, you will find this recipe very tasty. It's delicious with roast pork! I like to serve it hot, but have known some people who serve it cold. It has a sweet-and-sour flavor.

1 t. oil
4 slices bacon, cut into
    1/2-inch pieces
1 head green cabbage, cut into
    one-inch pieces

3/4 c. onion, thinly sliced
1/4 c. cider vinegar
1/4 c. sugar
3 T. soy sauce

Heat oil in a Dutch oven over medium heat. Add bacon; cook until crisp and golden, stirring often. Using a slotted spoon, transfer bacon to a paper towel; set aside. Add cabbage and onion to drippings in pan. Cook, stirring often, for about 10 minutes, until cabbage is wilted. Add remaining ingredients; cook for another 10 minutes. Stir in bacon and serve. Makes 6 servings.

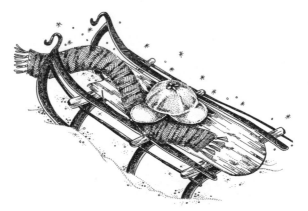

Throw an impromptu sledding party for the first snowfall! Gather friends & neighbors to enjoy some snow fun, and then head back home to a cozy fire and mugs of hot cocoa or mulled cider.

Christmas
Dinner
Together

Christmas Comfort Foods

Christmas Company Casserole

Sandy Coffey
Cincinnati, OH

This is a fun and tasty recipe that we enjoy over & over during the holidays. Can be made one day ahead to save time.

8-oz. pkg. egg noodles,
  uncooked
1 lb. ground beef
5 T. butter, melted and divided
2 8-oz cans tomato sauce
1 c. cottage cheese

8-oz. pkg. cream cheese,
  softened
1/4 c. sour cream
1/2 green pepper, chopped
1 T. green onions, chopped

Cook noodles according to package directions; drain. Meanwhile, in a skillet over medium heat, brown beef in 3 tablespoons butter. Stir in tomato sauce; remove from heat. In a bowl, combine remaining ingredients; mix well. Spread half of cooked noodles in a greased 3-quart casserole dish. Cover with all of cheese mixture; add remaining noodles. Drizzle remaining butter over noodles; spoon beef sauce on top. Bake, uncovered, at 350 degrees for 30 to 40 minutes, until hot and bubbly. Makes 6 servings.

Keep the Christmas dinner menu simple, familiar and yummy.
You may even want to ask your family ahead of time what dishes
are special to them. It's a day for tradition and comfort...
and you'll be more relaxed too.

Christmas Dinner
Together

Cheesy Pasta Skillet

Sandra Turner
Fayetteville, NC

This has been a favorite family dinner for years. I love that it is all done in one skillet and I can have dinner on the table in less than 30 minutes...perfect for all those busy days in December! Serve with a crisp tossed salad.

1 lb. ground beef
1 c. onion, chopped
14-1/2 oz. can diced tomatoes
   in sauce
1 c. water

1 T. Italian seasoning
1-1/2 c. ziti pasta, uncooked
1-1/2 c. shredded Cheddar
   cheese

In a skillet over medium heat, brown beef with onion; drain. Add tomatoes in sauce, water, seasoning and uncooked pasta; mix well. Cover and simmer over medium-low heat for 15 minutes, or until pasta is tender. Remove from heat. Top with cheese; cover skillet and let stand for 3 minutes, to allow cheese to melt. Makes 4 to 6 servings.

Skillet suppers are perfect for family meals after a day of Christmas shopping. For an easy side, whip up a marinated salad to keep in the fridge...cut up crunchy veggies and toss with zesty Italian salad dressing.

Christmas Comfort Foods

Trenton's Favorite Salsa Chicken

Katie Bissonette
Stamford, NY

What's better than a dump-and-go dinner? This slow-cooker recipe is perfect for low-key evenings or super-full schedules... it's my son Trenton's favorite!

16-oz. jar favorite salsa
15-1/2 oz. can black beans, drained and rinsed
15-1/4 oz. can corn, drained
1 onion, chopped
1-1/4 oz. pkg taco seasoning mix

2 c. shredded taco-blend cheese, divided
2 boneless, skinless chicken breasts
tortilla chips or tortillas

In a 5-quart slow cooker, combine salsa, beans, corn, onion, taco seasoning and one cup cheese. Mix well; add chicken and push gently into mixture. Cover and cook on high setting for 4 hours, or on low setting for 6 hours, stirring once, until chicken is very tender. Remove chicken and shred; return to crock and stir. To serve, ladle chicken mixture over tortilla chips or tortillas; top with remaining cheese. Makes 6 servings.

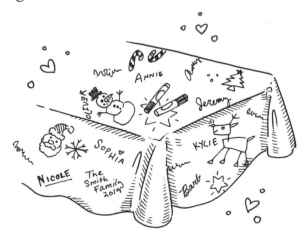

At holiday dinners, use a special tablecloth and ask family members, friends and special visitors to sign it with fabric markers. Sure to become a cherished tradition!

Christmas Dinner
Together

Donna's Taco Meatballs

Donna Wilson
Maryville, TN

I have made this recipe for my kids since they were younger. Whenever they had friends over, the friends all enjoyed these meatballs too...even had them asking for the recipe! It's so easy to make on a busy night and just pop in the oven. We usually have it with Mexican rice and a chopped salad.

1 c. biscuit baking mix
1-1/4 oz. pkg. taco seasoning
   mix
1 c. shredded Cheddar cheese

1/2 c. water
1 lb. ground beef
Garnish: salsa or taco sauce

Combine biscuit mix, seasoning mix, cheese and water in a large bowl; mix together well. Crumble beef over all; mix well and shape into meatballs by tablespoonfuls. Arrange meatballs in a lightly greased 13"x9" baking pan. Bake, uncovered, at 350 degrees for 15 to 20 minutes, until cooked through. Serve with salsa or taco sauce. Makes 6 servings.

For a sweet centerpiece, start with a glass-domed cheese platter.
Sprinkle mica flakes on the platter, add a toy vehicle topped
with a tiny bottle-brush "tree" and set it in the "snow."
Add the lid and it's done...so cute!

Christmas
Comfort Foods

Forgotten Chicken

Kathy Grashoff
Fort Wayne, IN

This recipe is the greatest! I have made it for people having surgery, new baby in the family and such. It's always requested by my in-laws when we have them over. It's a fantastic recipe to put together during the holidays, too...your family won't believe how delicious this is. Everyone loves the rice mixture on the bottom!

1 c. instant rice, uncooked
10-3/4 oz. can cream of
   chicken soup
10-3/4 oz. can cream of
   celery soup

10-3/4 oz. can cream of
   mushroom soup
3 lbs. chicken pieces
1.35-oz. pkg. onion soup mix

Spread uncooked rice in a greased 13"x9" baking pan; set aside. Mix soups in a microwave-safe bowl; microwave until hot. Spoon soup mixture over rice. Arrange chicken pieces on top; sprinkle with soup mix. Cover pan tightly with aluminum foil; set on a rimmed baking sheet to catch any drips. Bake at 350 degrees for 2-1/2 hours. Do not peek! Makes 4 to 6 servings.

Supreme Chuck Roast

Sandy Ward
Anderson, IN

Such a nice dish to cozy up to on a cold, wintry night! Tender and delicious, an elegant meal. Serve with mashed potatoes, steamed vegetables and warm bread.

3 to 4-lb. beef chuck roast
14-oz. bottle catsup
14-oz. can beef broth

1/2 c. brown sugar, packed
salt and pepper to taste

Place roast in a Dutch oven or a roasting pan with a lid; set aside. Mix remaining ingredients in a bowl; spoon over roast. Cover and bake at 325 degrees for 3 hours, or until roast is very tender. Remove roast to a platter; slice and serve. Makes 6 to 8 servings.

Christmas Dinner
Together

Pineapple–Orange Glazed Ham
Carolyn Deckard
Bedford, IN

This is a great way to fix a ham for family gatherings. With a slow cooker, it's really simple. Everyone always wants my recipe!

3 to 5-lb. boneless cooked ham
8-oz. can crushed pineapple in
   unsweetened juice, drained
   and juice reserved

1/2 c. brown sugar, packed
3 T. orange marmalade, divided
1 t. mustard

Place ham in a 5-quart slow cooker. Pour reserved pineapple juice over ham; refrigerate pineapple. In a small bowl, combine brown sugar, one tablespoon marmalade and mustard; mix well and spread over ham. Cover and cook on low setting for 6 to 8 hours. About 5 minutes before serving, in a small microwave-safe bowl, combine pineapple and remaining marmalade; mix well. Microwave on high for 1-1/2 minutes, or until heated through, stirring once halfway through cooking. Remove ham from slow cooker; place on a cutting board. Slice ham and serve with pineapple mixture. Serves 8 to 10.

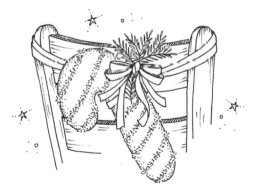

For a holiday look, thread red & white ribbon through mini wreaths and tie onto the back of each dining room chair.

Christmas Comfort Foods

Skillet Ravioli with Spinach

Kathy Grashoff
Fort Wayne, IN

*This dish is so easy and goes together quickly, using just a skillet.
Be warned...it may only serve 2 to 3 people, it was that good!
A crisp salad and crusty bread or garlic bread rounds it out.*

1 T. olive oil
2 cloves garlic, chopped
5-oz. pkg. baby spinach
1/2 t. salt, divided
pepper or red pepper flakes
    to taste

18-oz. pkg. refrigerated cheese &
    spinach ravioli, uncooked
1/2 c. water
6 T. mascarpone cheese
1/2 c. grated Parmesan cheese

In an oven-proof skillet over medium-high heat, heat oil with garlic.
Cook until garlic is barely golden, about 30 seconds to one minute. Add
spinach and 1/4 teaspoon salt; cook for 3 to 4 minutes, until spinach is
wilted. Season with pepper or red pepper flakes; transfer to a bowl and
set aside. Add uncooked ravioli, water and remaining salt to same
skillet. Bring to a boil over high heat; reduce heat to medium. Cover and
cook for 3 to 5 minutes, until ravioli is heated through and tender. Add
small spoonfuls of mascarpone cheese around ravioli; season with more
salt and pepper. Return spinach to pan; sprinkle with Parmesan cheese.
Heat a broiler rack 6 inches from heat; broil for 3 to 6 minutes, until
ravioli is browned in spots. Serve immediately. Serves 3 to 4.

Sing we all merrily, Christmas is here,
The day we love best of the days in the year.
–Old English carol

Christmas Dinner
Together

Garlic Shrimp & Rice

Stephanie Norton
Saginaw, TX

An elegant main dish that seems fussy without the fuss!

6-oz. pkg. long-grain and
   wild rice
1 T. butter
1/2 c. onion, chopped
1 c. sliced mushrooms

1 lb. medium shrimp, peeled
   and cleaned
minced garlic to taste
salt and pepper to taste

Cook rice according to package directions. Meanwhile, melt butter in a skillet over medium heat; sauté onion and mushrooms until soft. Add shrimp; cook until shrimp turns pink, but do not overcook. Add garlic, salt and pepper as desired. To serve, spread cooked rice on a platter; top with shrimp mixture. Serves 6 to 8.

Best Salmon Marinade

Amy DeLorme
Bellingham, WA

This recipe couldn't be simpler, and it is the most delicious flavor on salmon I have ever tasted! Most of the ingredients I already have on hand. Sometimes I'll put everything in a plastic zipping bag and refrigerate until I'm ready to cook.

1-1/2 lbs. salmon steak
1 c. orange juice
1/4 c. soy sauce
2 T. ginger root, peeled
   and minced

2 T. canola oil
1 T. honey
1 clove garlic, minced
salt and pepper to taste

Place salmon in a glass container; set aside. Combine remaining ingredients in a bowl; mix well and spoon over salmon. Cover and refrigerate for 15 minutes to one hour. Drain; place salmon on an aluminum foil-lined baking sheet. Broil about 4 to 5 inches from heat for 10 minutes per inch of thickness, until golden. Thinner steaks will take 5 to 7 minutes. Makes 4 to 6 servings.

Christmas
Comfort Foods

Chicken Tetrazzini

Carmen Hyde
Spencerville, IN

This recipe is fairly simple. We've also made Turkey Tetrazzini with leftovers after the holidays. I hope your family enjoys it as much as ours does.

16-oz. pkg. thin spaghetti, uncooked and broken into 3 to 4 pieces
3/4 c. plus 2 T. butter, divided
1 c. all-purpose flour
4 c. milk
1 t. garlic powder

2 10-3/4 oz. cans cream of chicken soup
3 c. shredded Cheddar cheese
4 c. cooked chicken, chopped
12 buttery round crackers, crushed

Cook spaghetti according to package directions; drain and return to pan. Meanwhile, in a large saucepan over medium heat, melt 3/4 cup butter. Sprinkle flour over butter; cook and stir until blended. Reduce heat to low. Add milk; cook and stir until thickened. Stir in garlic powder and soup; blend in cheese and chicken. Add chicken mixture to cooked spaghetti; mix well. Transfer mixture to a lightly greased 17"x11" baking pan. Melt remaining butter and combine with cracker crumbs; sprinkle on top. Bake, uncovered, at 350 degrees for 30 minutes, or until hot and bubbly. Serves 10 to 12.

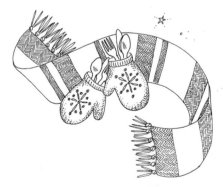

Lots of family members to buy for? Choose a single item like woolly knitted scarves or cozy winter slippers to buy for everyone, in different colors and textures.

Christmas Dinner
Together

Holiday Meatloaf

Carolyn Deckard
Bedford, IN

I love trying different meatloaves and this is one of my favorites. I like the meatloaf at everyone's favorite country-style restaurant, but I think this one is just as good! Makes great sandwiches too.

2 lbs. lean ground beef
1 lb. ground pork sausage
18 saltine crackers, crushed
1/2 green pepper, diced
1/2 onion, finely chopped
2 eggs, lightly beaten

1 T. Worcestershire sauce
1 t. mustard
1/2 c. brown sugar, packed
  and divided
1/2 c. catsup

In a large bowl, combine beef, sausage, crackers, green pepper, onion, eggs, Worcestershire sauce, mustard and 1/4 cup brown sugar. Mix just until blended. Form into a 10-inch by 5-inch loaf; place in a lightly greased 11"x7" baking pan. Bake, uncovered, at 350 degrees for one hour. Remove from oven; drain pan. In a small bowl, stir together catsup and remaining brown sugar; spoon over meatloaf. Bake another 15 minutes, or until a meat thermometer inserted into thickest portion registers 160 degrees. Remove from oven; let stand for 20 minutes. Turn meatloaf out of pan onto a platter and slice. Makes 10 servings.

Be sure to share family tales at Christmastime...they're super conversation starters. How about the time Grandma set out cookies to cool and her dog Skippy ate them, or the year a big snowstorm led to a houseful of extra Christmas guests? It's such fun to share stories like these!

Christmas
Comfort Foods

Mom's Chicken Enchiladas

Helen McKay
Edmond, OK

My mom made this recipe often for company and for our family dinners. It's easy and fast to put together. If you have leftover roast turkey from Thanksgiving or Christmas, you can use that.

4 boneless, skinless chicken
  breasts
2-1/4 c. cream of
  mushroom soup
1/2 c. milk
1-1/4 c. canned chopped
  green chiles

1-1/2 c. sour cream
1 bunch green onions, chopped
1/4 t. salt
1 doz. corn tortillas, divided
2 c. Longhorn cheese, shredded
  and divided

In a large saucepan, cover chicken breasts with water. Cook over medium heat until chicken is cooked through. Remove to a bowl; drain and chop. Meanwhile, in another large saucepan, whisk together mushroom soup, milk and chiles. Cook over medium heat until hot and bubbly; stir until smooth and remove from heat. Stir in chicken, sour cream, onions and salt. In a greased 13"x9" baking pan, layer half of chicken mixture, 6 tortillas and one cup cheese. Repeat layering. Bake, uncovered, at 350 degrees for one hour, or until bubbly and cheese is melted. Makes 8 to 10 servings.

A quick & tasty side for any south-of-the-border main dish!
Stir spicy salsa and shredded cheese into hot cooked instant rice.
Cover and let stand a few minutes, until cheese melts.

Christmas Dinner
Together

Grandma's Spaghetti Sauce

Emilie Britton
New Bremen, OH

*This makes a big batch! Perfect for simmering on the stove
all afternoon while you decorate the tree and wrap gifts.
Enjoy with your favorite pasta.*

1 to 2 T. oil
1 lb. beef chuck roast
1 lb. boneless pork roast
2 to 3 onions, chopped
12 c. water

4 6-oz. cans tomato paste
2 T. sugar
1 T. salt, or to taste
2 cloves garlic, chopped

Heat oil in a large skillet over medium-high heat. Brown roasts with onions on all sides. Transfer mixture to a large stockpot; add remaining ingredients. Bring to a boil over high heat; reduce heat to medium-low. Cover and simmer for 2 hours, stirring occasionally. Remove roasts to a platter; shred and return to pan. Uncover; reduce heat to low. Cook another 2 to 3 hours, stirring occasionally. Makes 8 to 10 servings.

Penne Carbonaro

Tiffany Jones
Batesville, AR

*This pasta is so delicious. We sometimes add grilled chicken for
a heartier meal, but it is scrumptious on its own.*

16-oz. pkg. penne pasta,
   uncooked
8 slices bacon, chopped
1/2 c. mushrooms, chopped
1/3 c. butter, cubed
1-1/2 c. half-and-half

1 t. dried parsley
1 t. garlic, minced
7 drops hot pepper sauce
1/2 t. salt
2/3 c. grated Parmesan cheese

Cook pasta according to package directions; drain. Meanwhile, in a skillet, cook bacon over medium heat until crisp. With a slotted spoon, remove bacon to paper towels; drain. Cook mushrooms in drippings; remove to paper towels. Drain drippings from skillet; add remaining ingredients except cheese. Cook and stir over medium heat until butter melts. Add cooked pasta to skillet. Stir in bacon, mushrooms and cheese; heat through. Serves 4.

Christmas Comfort Foods

Primavera Pasta & Veggies

Kathy Courington
Canton, GA

I make this whenever we want to have a lighter, meatless supper. So quick & easy and yummy, good any time of year. It's a recipe you can change around and add what you like...sometimes I will add cooked chicken and mushrooms.

3 c. bowtie or rotini pasta, uncooked
2 c. broccoli and/or zucchini, chopped or sliced
1 to 2 carrots, peeled and cut into thin strips

10-3/4 oz can cream of mushroom or chicken soup
1/2 c. milk
1/4 c. grated Parmesan cheese
1 clove garlic, minced
1/8 t. pepper

Cook pasta according to package directions; drain. Meanwhile, in a large saucepan, combine remaining ingredients; mix well. Cook, uncovered, over medium heat until vegetables are tender, about 10 to 12 minutes. Stir in cooked pasta and heat through. Makes 4 servings.

Do you have friends who live far away? Gather together your family and hold up a big sign that says "Merry Christmas!" Take a picture and send it to them, or share it online...they'll love it!

Christmas Dinner
Together

Vegetarian Fish Stew

Liz Plotnick-Snay
Gooseberry Patch

We have an older friend whose husband has been in & out of the hospital while she's working and caring for him. The best thing I could think to do for them was to make them a meal to cover two lunches or dinners. The difficult part is that they are pescatarian, but the fish must have fins and scales. Delivered with crusty bread, this recipe, modified to their tastes, came out perfectly!

3 to 4 new redskin potatoes,
   cubed
6 T. olive oil
1 onion, chopped
2 stalks celery, sliced
3 cloves garlic, minced
2/3 c. fresh parsley, chopped
14-1/2 oz. can no-salt-added
   crushed tomatoes
2 t. tomato paste
14-oz. can low-sodium
   vegetable broth

1 zucchini, quartered and sliced
1-1/2 lbs. cod fillets, cut into
   large chunks (or halibut,
   red snapper or sea bass)
1 t. salt
1/8 t. pepper
1/16 t. dried oregano
1/16 t. dried thyme
1/8 t. hot pepper sauce, or more
   to taste

In a small saucepan, cover potatoes with water; bring to a boil over medium-high heat. Cook for 10 minutes, or until almost soft; drain, rinse and set aside. Heat olive oil in a heavy stockpot over medium heat. Add onion and celery; sauté for about 4 minutes. Stir in garlic; cook for one minute. Stir in parsley; cook for 2 minutes. Stir in tomatoes with juice and tomato paste; cook for 10 minutes. Add vegetable broth, potatoes, zucchini and fish; bring to a simmer. Simmer until fish is cooked through and flaky, about 3 to 5 minutes. Add seasonings and hot sauce; stir and serve. Makes 4 to 6 servings.

Wide-rimmed soup plates are perfect for serving hearty dinner portions of stew as well as saucy pasta dishes. Add a slice of bread on the rim of the plate.

Christmas Comfort Foods

Sausage & Beans

Sandra Turner
Fayetteville, NC

This recipe has evolved over the years to suit my family's taste. It's requested so often during the cooler months that I have several paper tote bags fixed up with all the canned ingredients together. That way, I know I have everything I need and can fix dinner in minutes. Sometimes I will add an extra can of beans.

14-oz. pkg. smoked beef sausage or Kielbasa sausage, sliced into rounds
3/4 c. onion, diced
1 T. oil
10-oz. can diced tomatoes with green chiles

14-1/2 oz. can diced tomatoes
8-oz. can tomato sauce
15-1/2 oz. can pinto beans, drained and rinsed
15-1/2 oz. can Great Northern beans, drained and rinsed

In a large stockpot over medium heat, cook sausage and onion in oil until sausage is lightly browned and onion is tender. Add tomatoes with juice, tomato sauce and beans to pot; bring to a boil. Reduce heat to medium-low; simmer until heated through. If a thinner consistency is desired, stir in a little water. Makes 4 to 6 servings.

Tuck Christmas cards into a vintage napkin holder as they arrive in your mailbox...share greetings from friends and relatives over dinner each day.

Christmas Dinner
Together

Party-Time Pork Chops

Lois Hobart
Newcomerstown, OH

These pork chops are very tasty and have a little bit of Asian flair to them. They go nicely with cooked rice or potatoes and a zesty salad.

8 bone-in pork chops
6 T. oil, divided
1/4 c. soy sauce
1 clove garlic, minced
3/4 t. ground ginger

1/4 t. dried oregano
1 T. pure maple syrup
3/4 c. sherry, white cooking wine
   or apple juice

In a large skillet over medium heat, brown pork chops in 2 tablespoons oil. Transfer pork chops to a lightly greased 13"x9" baking pan; set aside. In a blender, combine remaining oil and other ingredients. Process until smooth, about 15 seconds. Pour mixture over pork chops. Bake, uncovered, at 350 degrees for one to 1-1/2 hours, turning pork chops once while baking, until tender. Makes 8 servings.

Giving a large, hard-to-wrap gift this year? Just hide it around the house. Wrap up a smaller gift...for example, a bicycle bell for a new bike or a tiny doll for a dollhouse. Tie on a gift tag hinting at where to look for the large gift. Half the work and twice the fun!

Christmas Comfort Foods

Cream Cheese–Stuffed Chicken

Jessica Payne
Springville, TN

*I love to make this recipe. It is by far one of my favorites...
so easy, and super delicious! The bacon drippings cook out
and keep the chicken moist and tender.*

8 boneless, skinless chicken
    thighs
8-oz. pkg. cream cheese,
    softened
1 T. Italian seasoning

1 t. garlic powder
1 t. onion powder
8 thick-cut slices bacon
Garnish: paprika

Place each piece of chicken between 2 pieces of plastic wrap; flatten
with a meat mallet and set aside. Mix cream cheese and seasonings in a
small bowl. Spread mixture onto the insides of chicken pieces. Roll up
each piece of chicken; wrap with a slice of bacon rolled from one end to
the other. Secure bacon with wooden toothpicks at both ends. Arrange
chicken in a lightly greased 8"x8" baking pan; will be a tight fit. Bake,
uncovered, at 350 degrees for about 30 minutes. Makes 4 servings.

It's fun to mix & match...set a festive table with items you
already have! Green transferware serving bowls and jadite cake
stands, sparkling white china dinner plates and ruby-red stemmed
glasses combine beautifully with Christmas dinnerware.

Christmas Dinner
Together

One-Pot Almond Chicken

LaDeana Cooper
Batavia, OH

I make this dish whenever I learn at the last minute that we're having guests. It only takes 30 minutes and everyone raves about how delicious it is.

8 boneless, skinless chicken
   thighs
1/4 c. zesty Italian salad dressing
1 c. chicken broth

2 c. green beans, trimmed
   and halved
1 c. instant rice, uncooked
1/4 c. sliced almonds

Combine chicken and salad dressing in a plastic zipping bag. Seal bag; set aside for several minutes. Transfer chicken and dressing to a large non-stick skillet. Cook over medium-high heat for 4 minutes on each side, or until golden. Stir in chicken broth; bring to a boil. Cover and simmer for 10 minutes. Add beans; cook for 5 minutes, or until chicken is cooked through. Remove chicken from skillet; add rice and almonds. Remove from heat. Cover and let stand for 5 minutes. Serve chicken over rice mixture. Makes 4 servings.

Holiday Cranberry Chicken

Jill Ball
Highland, UT

Nothing says the holidays like cranberries! This is one of our favorite dinners, and it's so easy to put together in a slow cooker. If you use chicken wings instead of breasts, it also makes a tasty party appetizer.

4 boneless, skinless chicken
   breasts
15-oz. can whole-berry
   cranberry sauce

1.35-oz. pkg. onion soup mix
8-oz. bottle Catalina or Russian
   salad dressing

Place chicken in a 4-quart slow cooker. Cover and cook on high setting for 3 hours, or until chicken is tender. In a bowl, mix remaining ingredients and spoon over chicken. Cover and cook on high setting for 30 more minutes. Makes 2 to 4 servings.

Christmas
Comfort Foods

Seafood Au Gratin

Paula Marchesi
Auburn, PA

We often make this delicious dish for family gatherings, holidays and special occasions. Born and raised on the eastern end of Long Island, New York, surrounded by beautiful waters, I love all kinds of seafood. Growing up, we ate fish at least four times a week. This is one of my favorites.

4 T. butter, divided
2 T. all-purpose flour
1/8 t. pepper
1 c. chicken or vegetable broth
1/2 c. milk
1/2 c. grated Parmesan cheese, divided
1-1/2 c. sliced mushrooms
1/2 lb. cooked sea scallops

1/2 lb. cooked small or medium shrimp, peeled and cleaned
1/2 lb. fresh or imitation crabmeat, shredded
1/2 c. shredded mozzarella cheese
1/2 c. shredded white Cheddar cheese
1 t. fresh parsley, minced

In a large saucepan over medium heat, melt 2 tablespoons butter. Stir in flour and pepper until smooth; gradually stir in broth and milk. Bring to a boil; cook and stir for 2 minutes, or until thickened. Stir in 1/4 cup Parmesan cheese; set aside. In a small skillet over medium heat, sauté mushrooms in remaining butter until tender; stir into cheese sauce. Arrange scallops, shrimp and crabmeat in a greased 11"x7" baking pan; spoon sauce over the top. Sprinkle with mozzarella cheese, Cheddar cheese, remaining Parmesan cheese and parsley. Bake, uncovered, at 350 degrees for 15 to 25 minutes, until bubbly and cheese is melted. Serves 6.

Christmas Day is a day of joy and charity.
May God make you very rich in both.
–Phillips Brooks

Fancy Stovetop Salmon Casserole

Laura Witham
Anchorage, AK

I'm always looking for new ways to feed the family, yet still keep things interesting. After a little research on methods and some trial & error, I created this super-yummy and easy recipe!

3 6-oz. salmon fillets
1 to 2 T. olive oil
2 t. lemon pepper
1 t. dried dill weed
1 t. onion powder
1/2 t. garlic powder

1 t. salt
15-oz. jar Alfredo sauce
2 c. chicken broth
16-oz. pkg. farfalle pasta, uncooked
4-oz. jar capers, drained

Arrange salmon fillets on an aluminum foil-lined baking sheet; lightly drizzle with olive oil. Combine all seasonings in a cup; sprinkle evenly over salmon. Cover salmon on baking sheet with foil; crimp sides all around to make a package. Bake at 350 degrees for 20 minutes. Meanwhile, on the stovetop in a large skillet or stockpot, combine Alfredo sauce and chicken broth; bring to a simmer. Add uncooked pasta. Cover and simmer over medium-low heat, stirring occasionally, for 20 minutes. Once salmon is done, remove from oven, uncover and flake with a fork. Gently mix salmon and capers into cooked pasta and serve. Makes 4 to 6 servings.

Give frozen ready-to-bake dinner rolls a homemade touch. Before baking, brush rolls with egg, beaten with a little water. Sprinkle with sesame seed or coarse salt and bake as usual.

Christmas
Comfort Foods

Best-Ever Cubed Steak

Teresa Carter
Wallace, NC

An easy, no-fuss, delicious recipe for slow cooker that your family & friends will rave about. Great for a crowd!

3 to 4 lbs. beef cubed steak
1-oz. pkg. ranch salad
   dressing mix
1-oz. pkg. Italian salad
   dressing mix

.87-oz. pkg. brown gravy mix
2-1/4 c. water, divided
Optional: 1/4 c. cornstarch
   or flour
mashed potatoes or cooked rice

Place cubed steak in a crockpot; sprinkle mixes on top. Pour in 2 cups water. Cover and cook on high setting for 3 to 4 hours, or on low setting for 7 to 8 hours, until steak is tender. Remove steak to a platter; cover to keep warm. If gravy is desired, blend flour or cornstarch and remaining water in a cup to make a smooth paste. Add to cooking liquid in slow cooker; stir well. Cover and cook on high setting for 15 minutes, or until mixture boils. Serve steak and gravy over mashed potatoes or cooked rice. Makes 6 to 8 servings.

On Christmas, younger family members may be too busy playing with new toys to enjoy a sit-down dinner. Instead, set out a buffet of sliced ham, baked beans, potato salad, fruit salad, rolls and bread, and a platter of Christmas cookies for dessert. Everyone can "graze" as they like.

Christmas Dinner
Together

Glazed Pork Tenderloin

Nancy Rollag
Kewaskum, WI

I have made this recipe for holidays and company for many years. It's easy and delicious, and everyone seems to love it.

2 1-1/2 lb. pork tenderloins,
   trimmed
1/2 c. currant jelly
1 T. grated horseradish, drained

1/2 c. chicken broth
1/4 c. Rhine wine, sweet white
   wine or apple juice
salt and pepper to taste

Place pork tenderloins on a wire rack in a shallow roasting pan; set aside. Combine jelly and horseradish in a microwave-safe cup. Microwave on high for one minute, or until jelly is melted; stir well. Brush half of jelly mixture over pork. Bake, uncovered, at 325 degrees for 30 minutes. Turn over and brush with remaining jelly mixture. Bake another 30 to 40 minutes, until a meat thermometer inserted in thickest part reads 150 degrees. Transfer pork to a cutting board; tent with aluminum foil and let stand for 10 minutes. Remove rack from pan; add broth and wine or juice to cooking juices in pan. Set pan over stove burners. Cook over medium-high heat for 4 to 5 minutes, until mixture is reduced to 1/2 cup, stirring often and scraping up any browned bits. Strain sauce; season with salt and pepper. Slice pork thinly and serve with sauce. Serves 6.

Homemade applesauce is a natural partner for pork, and it's easy to make. Peel, core and chop 4 tart apples and place in a saucepan with 1/4 cup brown sugar, 1/4 cup water and 1/2 teaspoon cinnamon. Cook over medium-low heat for 8 to 10 minutes, until soft. Mash with a potato masher and serve warm.

Christmas
Comfort Foods

Beef Wellington Loaves

Eleanor Dionne
Beverly, MA

*My friend Connie shared this recipe many years ago. She would
make it at Christmastime and take to parties. Since then,
I've made it one of my favorites for the holidays.*

2 eggs, beaten
2 10-3/4 oz. cans golden
   mushroom soup, divided
1/2 c. fine dry bread crumbs
1/2 c. onion, finely chopped
1 t. salt
1/4 t. pepper

2 lbs. lean ground beef
8-oz. tube refrigerated
   crescent rolls
1 c. water
2 T. fresh parsley, snipped
cooked rice

In a bowl, combine eggs, 1/2 cup soup, bread crumbs, onion, salt
and pepper. Add beef and mix well. Shape mixture into 2 loaves, each
6 inches by 3 inches. Place in an ungreased shallow 13"x9" baking pan.
Bake, uncovered, at 350 degrees for 55 to 60 minutes; spoon off
drippings in pan. Separate crescent rolls into 4 rectangles; press to seal
perforations. Place 2 rectangles of dough crosswise over the top and
down the sides of each loaf, overlapping slightly. Bake until dough is
golden, 15 to 20 minutes longer. In a small saucepan, whisk together
remaining soup, water and parsley; heat to boiling. Serve sauce with
loaves and cooked rice. Makes 8 servings.

Set the mood with jolly Christmas music! Ask guests to bring
along their favorites for a festive variety all evening long.

Christmas Dinner
Together

Sheet Pan Rosemary Chicken

Jackie Smulski
Lyons, IL

*This scrumptious chicken bakes up golden on a sheet pan. For an
easy side, coat spears of broccolini in the oil mixture;
add to pan about 15 minutes before chicken is done.*

3 to 4 lbs. chicken pieces
1 red or white onion, cut into
   thin wedges
1 lemon, sliced
6 to 8 cloves garlic, minced

4 sprigs fresh rosemary
1/4 c. extra-virgin olive oil
1/2 t. salt
1/2 t. pepper

In a large bowl, combine chicken pieces, onion, lemon, garlic and
rosemary sprigs. Drizzle with oil. Season with salt and pepper; toss to
coat. Arrange chicken on a lightly oiled 15"x10" jelly-roll pan; top with
remaining mixture from bowl. Bake, uncovered, at 400 degrees for
40 to 45 minutes, until chicken juices run clear and a meat thermometer
reads 170 degrees. Makes 4 to 6 servings.

For charming rustic placecards to set on dinner plates, write names
on small tags, punch a hole in one corner and slip the hole over
the stem of a fresh apple or pear.

Christmas Comfort Foods

Kielbasa & Shrimp with Rice

Karen Adams
Galax, VA

This is a quick & easy recipe that everyone enjoys. Just add a crisp tossed salad and some crusty bread for a delicious meal.

28-oz. can diced tomatoes
6-oz. pkg. long-grain and
  wild rice mix
2 c. water
14-oz. pkg. Kielbasa sausage,
  sliced

3/4 c. onion, chopped
15-1/2 oz. can pinto or Great
  Northern beans, drained
  and rinsed
1 lb. frozen cooked medium
  shrimp, thawed

In a large saucepan over medium-high heat, combine tomatoes with juice, rice with seasoning mix and water. Bring to a boil; reduce heat to medium and simmer for 25 minutes, or until rice is tender. Meanwhile, in a skillet over medium heat, brown sausage with onion. Add sausage mixture and beans to cooked rice mixture; heat through. Add shrimp; heat through and serve. Makes 8 servings.

Keep frozen shrimp on hand for delicious meals anytime. Thaw it overnight in the fridge, or if you're in a hurry, place the frozen shrimp in a colander and run ice-cold water over it. Don't thaw shrimp in the microwave, as it will get mushy.

Christmas Dinner
Together

Lemon-Parmesan Tilapia

Regina Vining
Warwick, RI

This fast recipe is perfect for Christmas Eve, when our family shares the Feast of the Seven Fishes.

2-1/2 lbs. tilapia fillets
2 t. butter, softened
2 T. plus 2 t. lemon juice, divided
1 c. mayonnaise

1/2 c. grated Parmesan cheese
Garnish: lemon wedges, fresh
  parsley

Rinse fish fillets in cold water; drain and pat dry. Place fish on a broiler pan; top with butter and 2 teaspoons lemon juice. Broil 4 inches from heat for 5 to 6 minutes, until fish is opaque and flakes easily with a fork. Remove from oven. Combine mayonnaise, cheese and remaining lemon juice; spoon evenly over fish. Broil another 2 to 3 minutes, until sauce puffs and turns golden. Arrange fish on a serving plate; garnish as desired. Makes 6 servings.

Spicy Flounder

Lisa Ann Panzino-DiNunzio
Vineland, NJ

One word...yum! Very easy to double for more servings.

1 lb. flounder fillets
1 T. olive oil
juice of 1/2 lemon

1 t. seafood seasoning, divided
Garnish: lemon wedges

Place fish fillets on a broiler pan coated with non-stick cooking spray. Brush with olive oil; squeeze lemon juice over fish. Sprinkle with half of seasoning. Broil 3 for 4 minutes; turn fish over. Add remaining seasoning. Broil for an additional 3 to 4 minutes, until fish flakes easily with a fork. Serve with lemon wedges. Makes 2 servings.

Need a quick, tasty side? Stir sautéed onion or celery
into prepared wild rice mix for a homemade touch.

Christmas
Comfort Foods

Pat's Holiday Lasagna

Pat Corneau
Salem, MA

Red and green peppers give this a holiday touch, but we enjoy it all year long! My family asks for this for all family gatherings.

8-oz. pkg. cream cheese, room
   temperature
16-oz. container sour cream
2 cloves garlic, minced
1 T. olive oil
1/2 c. onion, finely diced
1/2 c. red pepper, chopped
1/2 c. green pepper, chopped

1/2 c. mushrooms, chopped
1 lb. ground beef
48-oz. jar marinara sauce
9-oz. pkg. no-cook lasagna
   noodles, uncooked
16-oz. pkg. shredded mozzarella
   cheese, divided

In a bowl, blend cream cheese and sour cream; set aside. In a large skillet over medium heat, sauté garlic in olive oil until tender. Add onion and peppers; sauté until tender. Add mushrooms; cook until tender. Add beef; cook until browned and drain. Stir in marinara sauce; simmer for 15 minutes. Spoon a small amount of sauce into the bottom of a greased 13"x9" baking pan. Layer 4 uncooked noodles over sauce; spoon 1/3 of cream cheese mixture over noodles. Add enough sauce to cover this layer; top with a thin layer of mozzarella cheese. Repeat layering 2 more times, ending with noodles on top. Spoon remaining sauce over noodles. Cover with aluminum foil. Bake at 375 degrees for one hour. Remove foil; top with remaining mozzarella cheese. Bake for another 15 minutes, or until bubbly. Let stand for 10 minutes; cut into squares. Makes 10 to 12 servings.

Yummy garlic bread for a pasta dinner! Blend 1/2 cup softened butter, 1/4 teaspoon garlic powder and one teaspoon dried parsley; refrigerate until needed. To serve, spread on sliced Italian bread, reassemble loaf and wrap in foil. Bake at 400 degrees for 15 to 20 minutes.

Christmas Dinner
Together

7-in-One Tamale Dish

Jennifer Hatridge
Springfield, ME

My grandmother often made this dish for family gatherings.
Seven simple ingredients, brought together to make one tasty,
hearty dish that everyone loved!

12-oz. pkg. rotini pasta,
  uncooked
1 lb. ground beef
2 15-oz cans beef tamales
  in chili sauce, cut into
  one-inch pieces

14-3/4 oz. can creamed corn
8-oz. can tomato sauce
6-oz. can mushroom steak sauce
4-1/2 oz. can chopped black
  olives, drained

Cook pasta according to package directions, just until tender; drain.
Meanwhile, brown beef in a skillet over medium heat; drain. In a large
bowl, combine cooked pasta, beef and remaining ingredients; gently
mix together. Spoon into a greased 2-quart casserole dish. Cover and
bake at 350 degrees for one hour, or until hot and bubbly. Makes 8 to
10 servings.

Hosting a crowd for dinner? Serve festive Mexican, Italian or
Asian-style dishes that everybody loves. They usually feature rice or
pasta, so they're filling yet budget-friendly. The theme makes it
a snap to put together the menu and festive table decorations too.

Christmas Comfort Foods

Scalloped Potatoes & Ham

Dawn Van Horn
Columbia, NC

We southerners love our comfort food! This recipe is one that sticks to the ribs, especially on cold winter nights. Whenever you want something different after the holidays, it's a great way to use up leftover ham. For a change, I have also used pasta instead of potatoes...kids will love it either way!

2 T. onion, chopped
1/4 c. butter
1/4 c. all-purpose flour
1/2 t. dry mustard
1 t. salt
1/8 t. pepper

1-1/2 c. milk
2 c. shredded Cheddar cheese, divided
6 c. potatoes, peeled, cooked and sliced
1-1/2 c. cooked ham, cubed

In a skillet over medium heat, sauté onion in butter. Blend in flour, mustard, salt and pepper. Gradually add milk, stirring constantly until thickened. Mix in 1-1/2 cups cheese and stir until melted. Remove from heat; add potatoes and toss to coat. Spoon mixture into a greased 13"x9" baking pan. Arrange ham on top; sprinkle with remaining cheese. Bake, uncovered, at 350 degrees for 30 minutes, or until hot and bubbly. Serves 6.

Set a playful kiddie table...the children will beg to sit there!
Cover the tabletop with giftwrap, decorate paper cups and napkins
with holiday stickers and add a gingerbread house centerpiece.

Christmas Dinner
Together

No-Peek Christmas Eve
Beef Casserole

Marcia Shaffer
Conneaut Lake, PA

Got a lot to do to get ready for Christmas?
Pop this great dish in the oven!

2 lbs. stew beef cubes
10-3/4 oz. can cream of
   mushroom soup
1.35-oz. pkg. onion soup mix

8-oz. can sliced mushrooms,
   drained
1/2 c. water

Combine all ingredients in a greased 2-quart casserole dish; mix gently. Cover tightly. Bake at 300 degrees for 3 hours. Makes 6 servings.

Slow-Cooked Turkey Breast

Beckie Apple
Grannis, AR

Take it easy! Let your turkey breast slow-cook while you're busy
with the rest of the meal. You will have a nice amount of
turkey broth that will cook out to use for making gravy, too.

5 to 6-lb. turkey breast, thawed
   if frozen
1/4 c. margarine, melted

1 t. seasoned salt
1/4 t. pepper

Remove gravy packet from turkey breast, if packed with one. Add a plastic liner to a 5-quart slow cooker; pat turkey breast dry. Place breast-side up in slow cooker. Drizzle with melted margarine; sprinkle with seasonings. Cover and cook on high setting for 4 to 5 hours, until a meat thermometer inserted in the thickest part reads 165 degrees. Remove turkey to a platter; let stand several minutes before carving. Serves 6.

Christmas
Comfort Foods

Chow Mein Hotdish

Sharon Taylor
Bloomington, MN

Every Christmas Eve, for more years than I care to think about,
my mom served this for dinner. I have made it every year since she
passed away, and plan to pass the recipe on to the next group of kids.

1 lb. ground beef
1 c. celery, diced
1 c. onion, diced
2-1/4 c. water, divided
1 to 2 t. soy sauce
10-3/4 oz. can cream of
   mushroom soup

10-3/4 oz. can cream of
   chicken soup
4-oz. can sliced mushrooms,
   drained
8-oz. pkg. chow mein noodles,
   divided

Brown beef in a skillet over medium heat; drain. Add celery, onion
and one cup water. Cover and simmer for 15 minutes. Add soy sauce,
soups, remaining water and mushrooms. Stir in one cup chow mein
noodles. Top with another cup of noodles. Bake, uncovered, at
350 degrees for one hour. Serve with remaining noodles. Makes
6 to 8 servings.

A caroling party is a great time for everyone...don't worry if you
sing off-key, you'll be terrific! It's all about getting together
with friends and sharing the spirit of the season.

Christmas Dinner Together

Slow-Cooker Mexican Chicken

Lisa Barger
Conroe, TX

A very versatile recipe! It also makes a great taco filling or taco salad. I like to use 8 chicken breasts and extra jalapeño peppers.

6 to 8 boneless, skinless
    chicken breasts
24-oz. jar medium salsa
2 red peppers, sliced
1 onion, sliced
pepper to taste
juice of one lime
1 c. fresh cilantro, chopped

1-1/4 oz. pkg. taco
    seasoning mix
Optional: 2 jalapeño peppers,
    finely chopped, or more
    to taste
Garnish: sour cream, diced
    tomatoes, shredded Cheddar
    cheese

Place chicken breasts in a 6-quart slow cooker. Add remaining ingredients except garnish; do not stir. Cover and cook on low setting for 6 hours, or until chicken is very tender. Shred chicken. Serve topped with salsa mixture from slow cooker, as a taco filling or as a topping for taco salad. Garnish as desired. Makes 6 to 8 servings.

A dish filled with whole walnuts, almonds and hazelnuts is a treat for guests and can keep them busy while you put the finishing touches on dinner. Don't forget the nutcracker!

Christmas
Comfort Foods

Chicken & Broccoli Casserole

Mindy Wolfe
Warren, OH

This is a favorite comfort-food recipe that we always enjoy. It's a one-dish dinner...so good for busy days during the holidays.

16-oz. pkg. broccoli flowerets, thawed
3 boneless, skinless chicken breasts, cubed
16-oz. container sour cream
10-3/4 oz. can cream of chicken soup
1/4 c. milk
1/4 c. grated Parmesan cheese
1 t. garlic powder
1 t. paprika
1/4 c. butter
cooked rice

In a lightly greased 13"x9" baking pan, arrange broccoli flowerets in a single layer. Top with chicken; set aside. In a saucepan, combine remaining ingredients except rice; stir to combine. Cook over medium heat until heated through. Spoon over chicken and broccoli. Bake, uncovered, at 350 degrees for one hour. Serve over cooked rice. Makes 4 to 6 servings.

GREETINGS

The more the merrier! Why not invite a neighbor or a college student who might be spending the holiday alone to share in the Christmas feast?

Christmas Dinner
Together

Black-Eyed Peas & Ham

Tonya Sheppard
Galveston, TX

A must for luck on New Year's Day!

1 lb. dried black-eyed peas,
    rinsed and sorted
2 c. cooked ham, chopped
2 onions, diced
1/8 t. garlic powder
salt and pepper to taste
14-1/2 oz. can stewed tomatoes

Place peas in a large soup pot; add enough water to fill pan 3/4 full.
Stir in ham, onions and seasonings; set aside. Process tomatoes with
juice in a blender or food processor until liquefied; add to pan. Bring to
a boil over high heat; reduce heat to low. Cover and simmer for 2-1/2 to
3 hours, stirring occasionally, until peas are tender. Makes 14 to
16 servings.

Chicken & Gravy

Michele Eavey
Lafayette, IN

*A comforting recipe that's easy to toss together in a
slow cooker. This is thicker than your usual chicken &
noodles, and it's scrumptious.*

4 boneless, skinless chicken
    breasts
pepper to taste
2 .87-oz. pkgs. chicken
    gravy mix
10-3/4 oz. can cream of
    chicken soup
1/2 c. plus 2 T. water
1/2 of a 16-oz. pkg. egg noodles,
    uncooked

Season chicken breasts with pepper; place in a 4-quart slow cooker and
set aside. In a bowl whisk together dry gravy mix, soup and water.
Spoon mixture over chicken. Cover and cook on low setting for 4 to
6 hours, until chicken is very tender. Shred chicken in crock. Shortly
before serving time, cook noodles according to package directions; drain.
Add noodles to mixture in crock and stir. Makes 4 servings.

Christmas
Comfort Foods

Holiday Turkey Salad Sandwiches

Lori Rosenberg
Cleveland, OH

The last thing I want to do after a holiday is get back into the kitchen! So this easy recipe using leftover roast turkey meets the needs of a quick & easy and crowd-pleasing meal.

1 c. mayonnaise
1 t. paprika
1 t. seasoned salt
1-1/2 c. dried cranberries
   and/or raisins
1 c. celery, chopped

1/2 c. green pepper, minced
2 green onions, chopped
1 c. chopped pecans
4 c. cooked turkey, cubed
pepper to taste
sliced bread or split buns

In a large bowl, mix together mayonnaise, paprika and seasoned salt. Blend in cranberries or raisins, celery, green pepper, green onions and pecans. Fold in turkey and mix well; season with pepper to taste. Chill for one hour; spoon onto bread or buns and serve. Serves 12.

Leftover roast turkey freezes well for up to 3 months. Cut turkey into bite-size pieces, place in plastic freezer bags and pop in the freezer...ready to stir into hearty casseroles whenever you are.

Festive
Party Starters

Christmas Comfort Foods

Bacon & Caramelized Onion Dip

Virginia Campbell
Clifton Forge, VA

Our holiday get-togethers are casual, fun and filled with family, friends, and food! We set out a large table filled with treats and sweets and let everyone help themselves. This savory dip or spread usually goes first... it's hard to resist! Serve it with crackers, chips, cocktail bread slices, bread sticks, pita wedges, celery sticks, carrot sticks, broccoli and cauliflower flowerets, sweet pepper strips and whatever else you like.

1 lb. bacon
1 c. onion, chopped
16-oz. pkg. shredded mild or
    sharp Cheddar cheese,
    or a blend of cheeses

2 c. mayonnaise
1/2 t. garlic salt
1/8 t. cayenne pepper

In a large skillet over medium heat, cook bacon until crisp. Remove bacon to a paper towel-lined plate to drain; set aside. Add onion to hot bacon drippings in skillet; sauté until softened and beginning to turn golden. Remove onion with a slotted spoon; transfer to paper towels alongside bacon. Allow bacon and onion to cool. In a large bowl, combine cheese, mayonnaise and seasonings; mix well. Add crumbled bacon and onion; mix well. Cover and refrigerate until ready to serve. Makes 20 servings.

You've already trimmed the tree and beribboned the mantel... just add a welcoming row of twinkling luminarias along the front walk and your house will be party perfect!

Festive
Party Starters

Christmas Cereal Mix

Judy Phelan
Macomb, IL

Two to three weeks before Christmas, my husband and I deliver gift packages of this tasty snack mix to businesses that have helped us during the year. Instead of using mixed nuts in this, we like to make it extra-special with whole cashews.

4 c. crispy corn puff cereal
4 c. bite-size crispy corn & rice
   cereal squares
1/2 of a 16-oz. pkg. pretzel
   sticks
16-oz. can mixed nuts

1 c. butter, sliced
2 T. Worcestershire sauce
2 t. garlic salt
1 t. onion salt
1 t. celery salt

In a very large bowl, combine cereals, pretzels and nuts; mix well and set aside. Melt butter in a saucepan over medium heat, stir in remaining ingredients. Pour butter mixture over cereal mixture; stir to coat well. Spread mixture on an ungreased 15"x10" jelly-roll pan. Bake at 275 degrees for one hour, stirring every 20 minutes. Store in a covered container. Makes 20 servings.

Host a holiday movie marathon! Toss pillows and quilts on the floor, set out lots of snacks and have a non-stop viewing of all the best Christmas movies.

Christmas Comfort Foods

Susie's Clam Dip

Evelyn Thorpe
Lodi, CA

This recipe has been served at our family get-togethers every Christmas Eve for the past 30 years. It is my mother's favorite clam dip recipe, and it's great for parties. It's so good that once you try it, you will go back and back again! Plan on making a double batch. Mom always did, and there was never any left! It's delicious with ruffled potato chips.

2 8-oz. pkgs. cream cheese, softened
1 bunch green onions, green part only, chopped
juice of one lemon
2 shakes Worcestershire sauce
1 to 2 c. mayonnaise
6 6-1/2 oz. cans chopped clams, drained

In a large bowl, combine all ingredients except clams, adding mayonnaise to desired thickness. With an electric mixer on low speed, beat until all ingredients are combined. Add clams and stir well. Cover and refrigerate for 2 to 3 hours before serving. Makes 10 servings.

Be sure to mail Christmas and New Year's party invitations early enough to allow everyone time to RSVP.

Festive
Party Starters

Linda's Holiday Cranberry Salsa

Carolyn Deckard
Bedford, IN

When my sister Linda made this salsa for our family Christmas party, everyone hovered around the serving dish until none was left. The same thing happened when I took it to my office Christmas party. It's always a hit!

12-oz. pkg. cranberries, thawed
   if frozen
1 c. sugar
6 green onions, chopped
1/2 c. fresh cilantro, chopped

1 jalapeño pepper, seeded and
   finely chopped
8-oz. pkg. cream cheese, softened
assorted crackers or tortilla chips

Combine cranberries and sugar in a food processor; pulse until coarsely chopped. Transfer to a bowl; add onions, cilantro and jalapeño pepper. Mix well. Cover and refrigerate several hours or overnight. To serve, unwrap cream cheese and place on a serving plate. Drain salsa; spoon over cream cheese. Serve with crackers or tortilla chips. Makes 10 to 12 servings.

Write guests' names on shiny ornament balls with a gold glitter paint pen and heap them in a glass trifle bowl. They'll double as a tabletop decoration and as take-home gifts for everyone.

Christmas
Comfort Foods

Christmas Bruschetta

Jeannie Stone
Nova Scotia, Canada

We are a blended family and we always have a big crowd for Christmas. This recipe is an idea I had one Christmas when everyone was hungry. I doubled the recipe many times! Now it is a regular Christmas Eve treat for us.

1 baguette loaf, cut into 10 to
    12 slices
1 T. butter, melted
1/4 c. sweet onion salad dressing
3/4 c. dried cranberries
3/4 c. fire-roasted tomatoes,
    diced
3/4 c. shredded Parmesan cheese
Garnish: chopped fresh basil

Brush each baguette slice with melted butter; place on an ungreased baking sheet. Bake at 400 degrees for 2 to 3 minutes, just until beginning to toast. Remove from oven. Brush with salad dressing. Add cranberries and tomatoes; sprinkle with cheese. Return to oven for a few minutes, until toasted and cheese is melted. Add a little fresh basil. Makes 10 to 12 servings.

At Christmas, when old friends are meeting,
We give that long-loved joyous greeting...
Merry Christmas!
–Dorothy Brown Thompson

Festive
Party Starters

Alice's Meatballs

Tashia Stevens
Springvale, ME

*A coworker shared this recipe and I've made it my own
with the teriyaki sauce, garlic and sesame seed.*

1-1/2 lbs. ground beef
1 c. grated Romano cheese
1 egg, beaten
1 c. dry bread crumbs
1/4 c. milk

2 t. dried oregano
1/2 t. garlic salt
2 c. teriyaki sauce
2 T. garlic, minced, or to taste
2 T. sesame seed

In a large bowl, combine beef, cheese, egg, bread crumbs, milk, oregano
and garlic salt. Mix well; form into golfball-size meatballs. Brown
meatballs in a skillet over medium heat; drain. In a 3-quart slow cooker,
combine remaining ingredients; add meatballs. Cover and cook on low
setting for 4 to 6 hours, or on high setting for 2 to 3 hours. Serve with
toothpicks. Makes 10 to 20 meatballs.

Easy Cheesy Pull-Apart Bread

Liz Blackstone
Racine, WI

*Warm and ooey-gooey...stuffed with holiday flavors. Yum!
Use Swiss cheese, if you like.*

1 day-old round loaf Italian
   bread
3 c. Gruyère cheese, shredded
2 T. fresh thyme, minced

1/2 c. sweetened dried
   cranberries
1/4 c. butter, melted
salt and pepper to taste

Without cutting through the bottom crust, make vertical and horizontal
slices in loaf, about one inch apart. Stuff cheese, thyme and cranberries
into slices in loaf. Drizzle with melted butter; season lightly with salt
and pepper. Wrap loaf in aluminum foil; place on a baking sheet. Bake
at 400 degrees for 15 to 20 minutes, until toasted and cheese is melted.
Unwrap carefully; serve warm. Serves 8.

Attach tiny, shiny ornament balls to long party picks
with craft glue, just for fun.

Christmas Comfort Foods

Mexican Spinach Dip

Lisa Barger
Conroe, TX

Delicious and easy to prepare...everyone loves it!
Serve with your favorite tortilla chips.

2 10-oz. cans diced tomatoes
   with green chiles, divided
10-oz. pkg. frozen spinach,
   thawed and drained
8-oz. pkg. cream cheese, room
   temperature
1/2 c. onion, diced

1/2 jalapeño pepper, seeded
   and chopped
1-1/2 c. shredded Mexican-blend
   cheese, divided
1/3 c. sour cream
1/4 t. ground cumin
1/2 t. chili powder

In a bowl, combine one undrained can and one drained can of tomatoes.
Add remaining ingredients, reserving 1/2 cup shredded cheese for
topping. Mix well. Spoon into a lightly greased 13"x9" baking pan.
Sprinkle reserved cheese on top. Bake, uncovered, at 350 degrees for
30 minutes, or until hot and cheese is melted. Serve hot. Makes 10 to
12 servings.

Pop up a fun gift for a special friend! Fill a big enamelware bowl
with bags of popping corn, popcorn salt, recipes for snackable
popcorn treats and a classic Christmas movie on DVD.

Festive
Party Starters

Baked Mushroom Dip

Vickie
Gooseberry Patch

A delicious warm dip that our guests love, and an easy make-ahead. Assemble it but don't bake, cover and refrigerate up to two days. Uncover and bake for serving.

2 T. butter
3 c. mushrooms, chopped
1 c. onion, finely chopped
1 clove garlic, minced
8-oz. pkg. cream cheese,
  softened and cubed
1/2 t. dried dill weed

1/2 t. seasoned salt
pepper to taste
1-1/2 c. shredded Pepper
  Jack cheese
1/2 c. mayonnaise
Optional: snipped fresh chives
baguette slices or pita chips

Melt butter in a large skillet over medium heat; add mushrooms, onion and garlic. Cook for 10 minutes, or until mushrooms are golden and liquid is evaporated. Reduce heat to low. Add cream cheese and seasonings; cook and stir until cream cheese is melted. Add shredded cheese and mayonnaise; mix well. Spread mixture in an ungreased 9" pie plate or shallow casserole dish. Bake, uncovered, at 350 degrees for about 30 minutes, until hot and bubbly. Garnish with chives, if desired; serve with baguette slices or pita chips. Makes about 2-1/2 cups.

Ho-Ho-Ho! Invite a local Santa to drop in during this year's family get-together. What a joy for all ages!

Christmas
Comfort Foods

Christmas Shopping
Reuben Squares

Lynda Hart
Bluffdale, UT

This recipe has become our family tradition to serve after an afternoon of Christmas shopping. It can be made ahead, covered, refrigerated and baked at serving time; add five minutes to baking time. Serve with potato chips and dill pickle spears.

1 c. biscuit baking mix
1/4 c. water
1/2 lb. thin-sliced deli corned
    beef, cut into strips
8-oz. can sauerkraut, drained

1/2 c. Thousand Island salad
    dressing
2 c. shredded Swiss cheese
2 t. caraway seed

In a bowl, combine biscuit mix and water. Stir until a soft dough forms; beat vigorously for 20 strokes. With floured hands, pat dough into a lightly greased 8"x8" baking pan. Arrange corned beef strips evenly over dough; set aside. In a small bowl, mix together sauerkraut and salad dressing; spread over corned beef. Sprinkle with cheese and caraway seed. Bake, uncovered, at 375 degrees for about 30 minutes, until cheese is golden. Cut into 6 squares and serve. Makes 6 servings.

Serve easy-to-handle foods and beverages at tables in several
different rooms around the house. Guests will be able
to snack and mingle easily.

Festive
Party Starters

Holiday Wassail

Elisha Nelson
Brookline, MO

Every Christmas Eve, the wonderful aroma of wassail fills my mom's kitchen. It's a tradition that we drink this in our favorite Santa mugs! Double the recipe for a holiday party.

1/2 gal. apple cider
2 c. pineapple juice
1-1/2 c. orange juice

3/4 c. lemon juice
2 4-inch cinnamon sticks
1 T. whole cloves

Add all ingredients to a large stockpot, enclosing spices in a spice bag, if desired. Simmer over low heat for 2 to 3 hours, to allow flavors to blend. Serve hot in mugs. Leftover wassail may be refrigerated for up to one week; discard spices before refrigerating. Makes about 12 servings.

Christmas tree farms sometimes offer rides in horse-drawn sleighs or wagons...take the family for a ride they'll never forget! Tuck in a thermos of hot cocoa or spiced cider for warming up along the way.

Christmas
Comfort Foods

Mom's Garlic Balls

Judy Henfey
Cibolo, TX

My mom would make batches of these on Christmas Eve and New Years Eve as an appetizer. Some nights, she'd make a large green salad to serve with them, and that would be our dinner. Depending upon the crowd she was feeding, sometimes she would sprinkle some crushed red pepper flakes over them. Either way, they are delicious!

1 lb. pizza dough, thawed
    if frozen
1/2 c. canola oil
2 cloves garlic, finely minced

1 t. dried parsley
2 to 3 shakes garlic salt
salt and pepper to taste

Allow dough to rise at room temperature. Using kitchen scissors, snip walnut-size pieces of dough; roll into balls. Place dough balls on a greased baking sheet. Bake at 400 degrees for 20 minutes, or until golden. Meanwhile, mix together remaining ingredients in a large bowl. Add baked dough balls to oil mixture, a few at a time; stir well to coat. Remove and place in a large serving bowl. Makes 2 to 3 dozen.

Show off Christmas photos from years past in a vintage wire card holder. Choose a theme like visits to Santa, pets in holiday costumes or kids around the Christmas tree. Family & friends will love taking a trip down memory lane with you.

Festive
Party Starters

Outrageous Olive Cheese Balls

Pat Beach
Fisherville, KY

You'll love these cheese balls with their unique taste! Be ready to share this recipe with your family & friends. Serve with crackers.

2 8-oz. pkgs. cream cheese, softened
2 c. shredded Cheddar cheese
1 c. chopped pecans
15 green olives, drained and chopped
2 T. olive juice, or to taste
2-1/2 oz. pkg. real bacon pieces

Mix together all ingredients except pecans and crackers; form into 2 balls. Roll cheese balls in desired amount of pecans. Serves 10 to 12.

Roasted Bacon–Stuffed Dates

Courtney Stultz
Weir, KS

I love simple recipes, especially for get togethers! This one features three easy ingredients and a whole lot of flavor. A little sweet, a little salty...it makes a great appetizer or dessert snack.

20 dates, sliced down one side and pitted
8-oz. pkg. cream cheese, softened
4 slices bacon, crisply cooked and crumbled
Optional: honey or sea salt

Place dates on a parchment paper-lined baking sheet. Bake at 350 degrees for about 8 to 10 minutes, watching carefully to avoid burning. Remove from oven; spoon cream cheese into dates. Top with crumbled bacon. If desired, drizzle with a little honey or sprinkle with a little salt. Makes 10 servings.

Welcome guests with the scent of the holidays. Combine water and a sprinkling of cinnamon and pumpkin pie spice in a kettle and set over low heat to simmer.

Christmas
Comfort Foods

Cranberry Chutney

Doreen Knapp
Stanfordville, NY

This is my go-to cranberry dish for Thanksgiving and Christmas, and I just love it! I usually double the recipe. It's incredible, spooned over a wheel of warm Brie cheese or served with crackers on a cheese board. Makes the house smell like Christmas with warm spices!

12-oz. pkg. fresh cranberries
1/2 c. golden raisins or currants
1 c. apple cider, apple juice or
    cranberry juice cocktail
1 c. sugar
1/2 c. brown sugar, packed
2 t. cinnamon

1-1/2 t. ground ginger
1-1/2 t. ground cloves
1/4 t. allspice
1 c. white onion, diced
1 c. Granny Smith apple, cored
    and diced
zest and juice of one orange

In a Dutch oven or heavy-bottomed saucepan, combine cranberries, raisins or currants, fruit juice, sugars and spices; stir well. Cook over medium heat, stirring often, until cranberries pop, about 15 minutes. Stir in remaining ingredients; reduce heat to medium-low. Simmer, uncovered, for 15 minutes, or until thickened. For best flavor, cover and chill overnight before serving. Makes 8 servings.

For a fun family present, have your parents' old
home movies transferred to easy-to-watch DVDs.
Everyone will love sharing memories!

Festive
Party Starters

Fried Chicken Wings

Aqsa Masood
Ontario, Canada

I came up with this recipe because chicken wings are our most favorite snack to munch on! It is easy and time-saving. The wings can also be grilled instead of frying them. Serve with garlic bread and hot pepper sauce, if you like.

4 lbs. chicken wings, separated
juice of 1/2 lemon
1 t. smoked or regular paprika
1 t. garlic powder
1/2 t. salt
1 t. pepper
oil for frying
1/2 to 3/4 c. barbecue sauce

Pat chicken wings dry with paper towels; place in a large container. Combine lemon juice and seasonings in a cup; mix well and toss with wings. Cover and refrigerate for 15 minutes to one hour. In a deep skillet, heat several inches oil to 375 degrees over medium-high heat. Add wings, a few at a time; cook for 8 to 10 minutes, until crisp and golden. Drain on paper towels for several minutes. Toss with barbecue sauce and serve hot. Serves 5 to 6.

Bacon-Wrapped Smoky Links

Julie Hynek
Two Rivers, WI

Everyone loves these! After they've tried one,
everyone requests the recipe, too.

14-oz. pkg. mini smoked
  sausages
1 lb. bacon, slices cut in half
3/4 c. brown sugar, packed

Drain sausages; pat dry. Wrap each sausage with one piece of bacon; fasten with wooden toothpicks. Place on a broiler pan; sprinkle with brown sugar. Bake, uncovered, at 350 degrees for 30 to 40 minutes, until bacon is crisp. Makes 8 to 10 servings.

For party menus, tried & true is best! Use simple recipes you know will be a hit, rather than trying new recipes at the last minute.

Christmas Comfort Foods

Holiday Salami Bread

Victoria Case
Marysville, OH

This is our must-have family recipe for tree-trimming night. It is easy to put together and absolutely delicious! I always make this recipe two loaves at a time for our three sons and their big appetites. The recipe can easily be halved for smaller families.

2 16-oz. loaves frozen
   bread dough
1 egg, beaten, divided
Italian seasoning to taste

1/2 lb. sliced salami, divided
1/2 lb. sliced Swiss cheese,
   divided

In the morning, place each loaf of frozen bread dough in a 9"x5" loaf pan sprayed with non-stick vegetable spray. Cover loosely with plastic wrap coated with non-stick spray. Set in a warm place; allow to thaw and rise for about 8 hours. Spray a baking sheet and your hands with non-stick spray; place one loaf on pan. With your fingers, spread out dough to completely cover pan. Brush with half of beaten egg; sprinkle generously with Italian seasoning. Arrange half of sliced salami over dough to cover, leaving a 2-inch border of dough uncovered at each edge. Layer Swiss cheese on top of salami in the same way. Beginning at one short edge, roll dough into a snug roll. Use egg to seal the edge. Place roll seam-side down on a sprayed 15"x10" jelly-roll pan. Repeat all steps with second loaf; place it on the same pan. Brush both loaves with egg; sprinkle generously with Italian seasoning. Bake at 350 degrees for 35 to 40 minutes, until cooked through. Toward the end of baking time, cover loosely with aluminum foil if browning too fast. Cool for 5 to 10 minutes; slice with a serrated knife. Makes 2 loaves, 8 servings per loaf.

From sliders to stromboli, sandwiches are great party fare.
Just add a selection of potato chips, gourmet mustards and
crisp pickles for a great meal everyone is sure to enjoy.

Festive
Party Starters

Mom's Cranberry Punch

Janice Schuler
Alburtis, PA

My mom always made this punch for Christmas. She used to make a green ice wreath with cherries to place in the punch bowl. The kids always felt so special drinking this punch, while the adults were drinking their grown-up beverages!

4 c. cranberry juice cocktail
4 c. pineapple juice
1-1/2 c. sugar

1 T. almond extract
2 qts. ginger ale, chilled

In a large pitcher, combine fruit juices, sugar and extract. Stir well until sugar dissolves. Cover and chill well. At serving time, pour into a punch bowl; slowly pour in ginger ale. Makes 30 servings.

Christmas Nuts & Bolts

Shirl Parsons
Cape Carteret, NC

This snack mix is very addictive! I used to make this yearly for friends at Christmastime and it was probably my #1 most-requested holiday item. Pack in decorative tins for gifts.

2 c. doughnut-shaped oat cereal
2 c. bite-size shredded
    wheat cereal
2 c. pretzel sticks
1-1/2 c. unsalted peanuts
1/4 c. margarine

1 T. Worcestershire sauce
1/2 t. onion salt
1/2 t. garlic salt
1/2 t. celery salt
1/2 t. paprika

In a large bowl, combine cereals, pretzels and peanuts; set aside. Melt margarine in a small saucepan over low heat; stir in remaining ingredients. Pour over cereal mixture; toss well. Spread mixture on a 15"x10" jelly roll pan coated lightly with non-stick vegetable spray. Bake at 250 degrees for one hour, stirring every 15 minutes. Cool; store in a covered container. Makes about 8 cups.

Alongside disposable punch cups, set a jar filled with marker pens. Guests can write their names on the cups, for less waste.

Christmas Comfort Foods

Granny's Cheese Biscuits

Janette Ketcham
Nassau Bay, TX

Our best-loved family tradition is the making of my mother-in-law Ruth's cheese biscuits. Although Granny passed away over 20 years ago, our tradition continues to this day. Our whole family forms an assembly line to make these tasty cheese crackers, then we eat them with tiny bottles of cola. These biscuits were also the traditional "cookies for Santa" when our children were younger. Now in their 30s, we still make them together. In 2021, with Covid-19 concerns, our daughter could not make it home for Christmas. So, we had an afternoon-long Zoom conference while she made her cheese biscuits in California and we made ours here in Texas.

2 lbs. extra-sharp Cheddar
   cheese, shredded
1 lb. butter
3-2/3 c. all-purpose flour
1/4 tsp. cayenne pepper
1 egg, beaten
1 c. pecans, finely chopped
salt to taste

In the bowl of a stand mixer, beat cheese, butter, flour and cayenne pepper with electric mixer on medium speed, using a paddle attachment, until a firm dough forms. (This can be done by hand, but the dough is very stiff.) Add a little more flour if needed to form a firm dough. On a floured surface, with lightly floured hands, roll out dough into logs, one inch in diameter. Roll logs in wax paper; refrigerate or freeze until ready to bake. At baking time, slice logs thinly into 3/8-inch slices; arrange on parchment paper-lined baking sheets. Brush with beaten egg; top each with 1/2 teaspoon pecans. Bake at 375 degrees for 8 to 10 minutes, until edges are lightly golden and egg wash has bubbled. Immediately season with salt while still on baking sheets; cool on a wire rack. Makes 4 to 5 dozen.

Live music makes any gathering extra special. Ask a nearby school to recommend a music student who would enjoy playing Christmas carols on guitar, violin or piano.

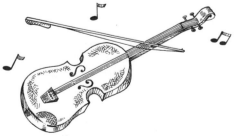

Festive
Party Starters

3-Cheese Party Cheese Ball

Bev Traxler
British Columbia, Canada

A very festive recipe that can be dressed up for any occasion!
I like to decorate this cheese ball with strips of pimento and
green pepper and sliced pimento-stuffed green olives.

2 8-oz. pkgs. cream cheese
1 c. shredded sharp Cheddar
   cheese
3/4 c. crumbled blue cheese
1/4 c. onion, minced
1 T. Worcestershire sauce

Place cheeses in a mixer bowl; let stand at room temperature until softened. Add onion and Worcestershire sauce; beat with an electric mixer on low speed until blended. Beat on medium speed until fluffy, scraping bowl often. Cover and chill at least 8 hours. Shape mixture into a large ball; place on a serving platter. Serves 10 to 12.

Cranberry Cheese Tarts

Sheri Kohl
Wentzville, MO

We love this recipe! The tarts look very festive on our Christmas
buffet table, and they disappear quickly. Fast and easy. Occasionally
we switch out the flavor of chutney, for a change.

2 1.9-oz. pkgs. frozen mini
   phyllo shells, thawed
8-oz. pkg. mozzarella cheese,
   cut into 1/2-inch cubes
1/3 c. cranberry chutney,
   divided

Place thawed phyllo shells on parchment-lined baking sheets. Add a cheese cube to each shell; top each with 1/2 teaspoon chutney. Bake at 400 degrees for 5 minutes, or until cheese melts. Serve warm. Makes 2-1/2 dozen.

If guests will be arriving at different times, keep hot dips
hot in a slow cooker set on low.

Christmas
Comfort Foods

Marinated Party Sandwiches

Ronda Hauss
Bluffton, SC

I first made these sandwiches several years ago for our Kentucky Derby party. Since then, I have been requested to make them for every occasion, from Christmas Eve buffets to graduation parties! At every gathering, there is at least one request for a copy of the recipe. This is easily doubled and tripled. Be sure to make extra, as they disappear fast. Yummy!

24 small dinner rolls, split
   and divided
1 lb. deli sliced roast turkey

12 slices Swiss cheese
1 lb. deli sliced baked ham
12 slices Cheddar cheese

Assemble 12 buns with turkey and Swiss cheese, folding turkey to fit buns; assemble remaining buns with ham and Cheddar cheese. Arrange sandwiches in an ungreased 13"x9" baking pan. Spoon Butter Sauce over sandwiches; cover and refrigerate overnight. Shortly before serving time, uncover. Bake at 350 degrees for 10 to 15 minutes, until bubbly and cheese is melted. Makes 24 servings.

Butter Sauce:

1/2 c. butter, sliced
2 T. brown sugar, packed
1 T. poppy seed

2 T. Worcestershire sauce
1 T. mustard

Combine all ingredients in a saucepan over medium heat. Cook, stirring constantly, until well blended.

Christmas decorations don't have to be all pine and holly! For a quick and casual centerpiece, curl a string of dried chile peppers into a circle, then set a hurricane with a fat red candle in the center.

Festive
Party Starters

Linda's Vegetable Dip

Barbara Lewis
Wellsburg, WV

My sister-in-law Linda made this dip for family at Christmas. I think I ate almost all of the veggies with this awesome dip...it is delicious!

8-oz. pkg cream cheese, softened
1/4 c. sugar
2 T. catsup
2 T. Catalina salad dressing
1 T. mayonnaise-style salad dressing
1 t. mustard
garlic salt to taste

Combine all ingredients in a large bowl. Using an electric mixer on medium speed, blend until smooth. Keep refrigerated. Serves 10 to 12.

Cracker Dip Dip

Pamela Johnson
Edmond, OK

When she was four years old, my daughter Hannah named this dip that I'd made for a business party. I usually make more than one batch, because it disappears quickly, especially when she is around. The longer it chills, the better it tastes.

5 green onions, chopped
8-oz. pkg. shredded Cheddar cheese
1-1/2 c. mayonnaise
1/2 c. real bacon bits
1/2 c. slivered almonds
club crackers or round buttery crackers

In a bowl, combine all ingredients except crackers; mix well. Cover and chill for at least 2 hours. Serve with your favorite crackers. Serves 4 to 6.

Add a warm glow to any holiday get-together with lots of twinkli~~ lights and candles. Battery-operated candles make it easy and s~

Christmas
Comfort Foods

Pepper Jack Cheese Ball

Shirl Parsons
Cape Carteret, NC

This is a sensational appetizer! Serve with crackers or tortilla chips.

1-1/2 c. shredded Pepper Jack
   cheese
1 c. shredded sharp Cheddar
   cheese
2 3-oz. pkgs. cream cheese,
   softened

1 T. lime juice
1/2 t. onion powder
1/4 c. sliced black olives, drained
1/4 c. fresh cilantro, chopped
3/4 c. nacho cheese-flavored
   tortilla chips, crushed

In a food processor, combine cheeses, lime juice and onion powder.
Process until well mixed; spoon into a bowl. Stir in olives and cilantro.
Place crushed tortilla chips on wax paper. Scoop out cheese mixture and
form into a ball; roll in chips to coat. Cover and chill until serving time.
Makes 8 servings.

Fill a big glass canister with wrapped candies and set it out
at your party...don't forget to count them first! Ask everyone
to guess how many candies are in the jar, then send it home
with the person whose guess is the closest.

Festive
Party Starters

Olive Muffin Pizza Appetizers

Georgia Muth
Penn Valley, CA

*My friend Lynn serves these appetizers at our frequent
neighborhood gatherings. They are always a hit!*

2-1/4 oz. can chopped black
  olives, drained
1/2 c. chopped green olives,
  drained
1-1/2 c. shredded Cheddar
  cheese

1/2 c. mayonnaise
1/2 t. chili powder
1/8 t. curry powder
1/4 t. salt
6 English muffins, split

In a bowl, combine all ingredients except muffins. Mix well; spread
on muffin halves. Arrange on an ungreased baking sheet. Broil until
bubbly, watching closely. Cut each muffin half into quarters; serve
warm. Makes 8 to 10 servings.

Use tiered cake stands for bite-size appetizers...so handy,
and they take up less space on the buffet table than
setting out several serving platters.

Christmas
Comfort Foods

Chilly-Day Cheese Spread

Sandy Jungkuntz
Schaumburg, IL

This recipe was created one weekend in northern Illinois when there was a wind chill warning on. Brrrr! We love crispy almond crackers with this spread.

8-oz. pkg. cream cheese, softened
1 c. shredded Italian-blend cheese
1/2 c. light mayonnaise
1 t. dried thyme
1 t. dried oregano

1 t. dried dill weed
1 t. dried basil
1 t. onion powder
1 t. garlic powder
1 t. garlic salt
1 t. pepper
snack crackers

In a bowl, mix together all ingredients except crackers. Cover and chill; the longer it chills, the stronger the flavor. Serve with your favorite crackers. Makes 2 cups.

If you have a favorite party recipe that calls for lots of different herbs or spices, measure them out into small plastic zipping bags and label. Later, when time is short, just pull out a bag and add it to your recipe.

Festive
Party Starters

J's Taco Dip

Diane Bertosa
Brunswick Hills, OH

Our family has been making this tasty and eye-appealing layered dip for over 30 years. Takes just a moment to fix, too.

2, 8-oz. pkgs. of cream cheese,
  softened
3/4 c. sour cream
10-1/2 oz. jar picante sauce
1/8 t. hot pepper sauce

1/8 t. garlic powder
Garnish: shredded lettuce,
  diced tomatoes, shredded
  Cheddar cheese
tortilla chips

In a bowl, blend cream cheese and sour cream well. Stir in sauces and garlic powder; spread mixture on a dinner plate. Sprinkle with shredded lettuce, then diced tomatoes and shredded cheese. Serve with tortilla chips. Makes 8 to 10 servings.

Taco Oyster Crackers

Thomas Campbell
Brooklyn Park, MN

This is something I love to make as gifts for the holidays. My friends request it every year. A single batch will give you three nice size treat bags.

9-oz. pkg. oyster crackers
1/2 c. oil

1-oz. pkg. taco seasoning mix

Place oyster crackers in a Dutch oven or a heavy baking pan. Blend together oil and taco seasoning; spoon over crackers. Stir carefully until crackers are well coated. Bake, uncovered, at 350 degrees for 15 minutes, stirring every 5 minutes. Spread on wax paper to cool. Store in an airtight container or divide into gift bags. Makes 6 to 8 servings.

May our house always be too small
to hold all of our friends!
–Myrtle Reed

Christmas
Comfort Foods

Bacon-Pecan Cheese Ball

Beckie Apple
Grannis, AR

When family & friends gather at the holidays, it's always good to have this cheese ball in the fridge for a tasty snack. But, we love it year 'round!

8-oz. pkg. cream cheese, softened
8-oz. pkg. shredded Cheddar cheese
1/2 c. finely chopped pecans

1/4 c. real bacon bits
2 T. mayonnaise
2 green onions, diced
1/4 t. garlic powder
snack crackers

In a large bowl, combine all ingredients except crackers. Mix well and form into a ball; wrap in plastic wrap. Refrigerate at least 2 to 3 hours; unwrap and place on a serving plate. Serve with your favorite crackers. Keeps for up to 2 weeks in refrigerator. Makes 6 to 8 servings.

For an easy yet elegant appetizer, try a cheese platter. Choose a soft cheese, a hard cheese and a semi-soft or crumbly cheese. Add a basket of crisp crackers, crusty baguette slices and some sliced apples or pears. So simple, yet sure to please guests.

Festive
Party Starters

Grandma's Chipped Beef Spread

Kimberly Redeker
Savoy, IL

Grandma always made this at Christmastime and shaped it into a standing snowman. I've also shaped it into stars, pumpkins and Easter eggs! It's a great seasonal dip.

2-1/4 oz. pkg. sliced dried beef,
   cut into tiny pieces
8-oz. pkg. cream cheese, softened
1 t. prepared horseradish

1/2 t. horseradish sauce
2 t. garlic powder, or more
   to taste

In a bowl, mix all ingredients together. Cover and chill until serving time. Serves 15 to 20.

Oven Chicken Dip

Sherry Noble
Paragould, AR

This dip is so good, you will want to double the recipe! If you'd like to add a little "kick" after baking, top with a few dollops of pepper jelly. Serve with crackers, chips or fresh vegetables.

12-1/4 oz. can white chicken,
   drained and flaked
8-oz. pkg. cream cheese,
   softened

8-oz. container sour cream
1/2 c. onion, diced
1/4 t. garlic salt
1 to 2 c. grated Parmesan cheese

In a large bowl, mix together all ingredients except Parmesan cheese. Spoon into a lightly greased one-quart casserole dish. Top with Parmesan cheese. Bake, uncovered, at 350 degrees for 30 to 40 minutes, until hot and bubbly. Makes 6 servings.

Set out a small discard dish for discarded toothpicks, to keep things tidy. Add one or 2 toothpicks in the dish so guests will get the idea!

179

Christmas
Comfort Foods

Reindeer Munch

Christina Burrell
North Richland Hills, TX

I love to give gifts! Nothing brings me more joy than finding or making the perfect gift for someone. During December, I especially love baking holiday treats to give to my neighbors, church friends, teachers and family. This is one of the most popular edible gifts I make! It's a fun holiday twist on a popular snack mix recipe. Pack in cute Christmas bags to give as gifts.

9 c. bite-size crispy corn, rice, wheat or chocolate cereal squares, or a combination
1 c. semi-sweet chocolate chips
1/2 c. creamy peanut butter
1/4 c. butter
1 t. vanilla extract
1-1/2 c. powdered sugar
10-oz. pkg. red & green candy-coated peanut butter chocolates

Add cereal to a large bowl; set aside. Combine chocolate chips, peanut butter and butter in a one-quart microwave-safe bowl. Microwave, uncovered, on high for one minute; stir. Microwave about 30 seconds longer, until mixture can be stirred smooth. Stir in vanilla. Spoon mixture over cereal, stirring to coat evenly. Pour into a 2-gallon plastic zipping bag. Add powdered sugar to bag. Seal bag; shake until well coated. Spread on wax paper-lined baking sheets to cool. Sprinkle chocolates over cereal mixture; stir to combine. Store in an airtight container in the refrigerator. Makes about 12 cups.

Pile everyone in the car for a trip around town to see the Christmas lights and decorations. Bring along some little bags of Reindeer Munch for snacking. Sweet memories in the making!

Festive
Party Starters

Sweet & Spicy Goodness Appetizer Dip

Kimtoiya Sam
Indianapolis, IN

My aunt was a wonderful hostess. Everyone's holiday parties started with her Sweet & Spicy Dip and crackers. It only takes a few minutes to make and it's delicious!

8-oz. jar peach or apricot
   preserves
1 T. Dijon mustard
2 to 3 T. grated horseradish

cracked pepper to taste
8-oz. pkg. cream cheese,
   softened
buttery round crackers or chips

In a bowl, whisk together preserves, mustard, 2 tablespoons horseradish and pepper. Add more horseradish, if desired. Cover and chill. To serve, unwrap cream cheese and place on a serving plate; spoon preserves mixture over cream cheese. Serve with crackers. Serves 8 to 10.

Christmas Teddy Bear Snack Mix

Diana Krol
Hutchinson, KS

Stir together this fun holiday snack mix for your favorite young friends. Serve it by the handfuls from a pretty bowl, or divide it into small bags to hand out to those you love.

10-oz. pkg. teddy-bear shaped
   graham crackers
15.4-oz. pkg. doughnut-shaped
   honey oat cereal

2 c. raisins
16-oz. jar honey-roasted peanuts
10-oz. pkg. seasonal candy-
   coated chocolates

In a large bowl, gently stir all ingredients together. Store in tightly covered container. Makes 8 to 10 servings.

Paper coffee filters make tidy toss-away holders for handfuls of snack mix.

Christmas Comfort Foods

Mascarpone Gingerbread Dip
Joslyn Hornstrom
Elgin, IL

When I was growing up, Mom always made gingerbread, served with a dollop of whipped cream. I was in heaven! The flavors in this yummy dip bring back so many childhood memories.

1/4 c. cream cheese, softened
8-oz. pkg. mascarpone cheese, softened
1/4 c. brown sugar, packed
1-1/2 T. molasses
1/2 t. cinnamon

1/2 t. ground ginger
1/8 t. ground cloves
1/8 t. nutmeg
Optional: small amount whipping cream or milk
cookies or graham crackers

In a bowl, beat cream cheese with an electric mixer on low to medium speed until smooth. Add mascarpone cheese; beat together until soft peaks form. Add brown sugar, molasses and spices; beat together until all ingredients are combined and mixture is fluffy. If dip is too thick, beat in a small amount of cream or milk to desired consistency. Transfer dip to a serving bowl; cover and refrigerate for several hours. Serve with cookies or graham crackers.

Fill an unused fireplace with 3 or 4 potted poinsettia plants for a splash of holiday color.

Sweet Treats
to Share

Christmas
Comfort Foods

Janet's Cran-Apple Crumbly

Janet Reinhart
Columbia, IL

I've been making Apple Crumbly for years, but love it even more now that I add cranberries for fall and winter. It's been a favorite of my husband's for over 20 years. It's delicious without cranberries too, but they make it so Christmasy. Easy to double in a 13"x9" baking pan. Serve with vanilla or cinnamon ice cream. Yum!

3 Gala apples, peeled, cored
　　and sliced
3 Granny Smith apples, peeled,
　　cored and sliced
1 c. fresh or frozen cranberries,
　　halved

1/4 c. sugar
1 T. cinnamon
1/2 c. butter, softened
1 c. brown sugar, packed
1/2 c. all-purpose flour
1/2 c. rolled oats, uncooked

Combine all apples in a large bowl; add cranberries. Toss to mix and set aside. In a small bowl, mix together sugar and cinnamon; spoon over fruit mixture and stir until coated. Transfer mixture to a buttered 9"x9" baking pan. In another bowl, combine remaining ingredients and mix until crumbly; spread over fruit mixture. Bake at 350 degrees for about 45 minutes, until apples are tender. Serve warm. Makes 8 to 9 servings.

Celebrate a snow day from school with a dessert party.
Sweet treats, along with plenty of time for sledding,
snowball fights and snowman building, will make for
a fun-filled afternoon!

Sweet Treats
to Share

Holiday Cut-Out Cookies

Karen Wald
Dalton, OH

At Christmas, this is our family's favorite cut-out cookie recipe. Sour cream is the key ingredient to these soft cookies.

1 c. butter, softened
1-1/2 c. sugar
3 eggs, beaten
1/2 c. sour cream
3-1/2 c. all-purpose flour
1/2 t. baking powder

1/2 t. baking soda
1/2 t. vanilla extract
1/8 c. boiling water
Garnish: favorite frosting
or glaze

In a large bowl, blend butter and sugar well. Add remaining ingredients except garnish; mix well. Cover and chill dough for at least 2 hours. Roll out dough on a floured surface, adding a little more flour, if too sticky. Cut dough into desired shapes with cookie cutters. Arrange on greased baking sheets. Bake at 375 degrees for 8 to 9 minutes; do not overbake. Remove to wire racks and cool; frost or glaze as desired. Makes 3 dozen.

Here's an easy trick to help cut-out cookie shapes bake up neatly. Place cookies on a parchment paper-lined baking sheet and pop into the fridge for 10 to 15 minutes, then bake.

Christmas Comfort Foods

Great-Grandma's Cherry Cookies

Shirley Brigman
Nickerson, KS

This cookie recipe was a family secret for 80 years or more. My aunt finally allowed it to be printed in our church's first cookbook, in honor of Grandma. The cookbook sold out, mainly from people wanting this recipe. Now I'm sharing it with you...I hope you love it too!

1 c. shortening
1 c. brown sugar, packed
1 c. sugar
2 eggs, beaten
1/2 c. milk
1 t. vanilla extract

3 c. all-purpose flour
1 t. baking powder
1 t. baking soda
1/2 t. salt
21-oz. can cherry pie filling

In a large bowl, blend together shortening and sugars. Add eggs, milk and vanilla; mix well and set aside. In another bowl, combine flour, baking powder, baking soda and salt. Add flour mixture to shortening mixture; mix well. Cover and chill dough, if too soft. Divide dough into 2 parts. Roll half of dough into balls the size of a large marble; place on greased baking sheets. With a floured thumb, make an indent in each ball; add 2 cherries and a little of the filling to each. Form remaining dough into flattened balls; place one on each filled cookie and press edges together. Bake at 350 degrees for 10 minutes, or until golden. Makes about 3-1/2 dozen.

Vintage flowered china plates can be picked up inexpensively at yard sales. They're just right for delivering cookies to a friend or neighbor...and there's no need to return the plate!

Sweet Treats
to Share

4-Ingredient Chocolate Chip Cookies

Cindy Neel
Gooseberry Patch

This recipe is so easy and tastes amazing! If you like peanut blossom cookies, you'll love these. The cookies do not change in appearance once in the oven, so the best way is to set a timer for 6 to 8 minutes.

1 c. crunchy or creamy peanut
  butter
1-1/2 c. sugar, divided
1 egg, beaten

1/2 c. semi-sweet chocolate chips
Garnish: additional sugar,
  chocolate chips

In a bowl, combine all ingredients except garnish; mix until smooth. Form dough into balls by tablespoonfuls; roll in additional sugar to coat. Place balls on baking sheets sprayed lightly with non-stick vegetable spray; press to flatten slightly. Top cookies with additional chocolate chips. Bake at 350 degrees for 6 to 8 minutes, until lightly golden on the bottom. Remove from oven. Cool slightly, remove cookies to paper towels to cool. Store in an airtight container. Makes 2 to 3 dozen.

Simple Coconut Macaroons

Lisa Burger
Conroe, TX

I have used this recipe for years...it's the easiest macaroon recipe ever! If you wish to drizzle chocolate on top, make sure the cookies have cooled first.

14-oz. can sweetened condensed
  milk

14-oz. pkg. flaked coconut
1 t. vanilla extract

Combine all ingredients in a bowl; mix well. Drop by teaspoonfuls onto parchment paper-lined baking sheets. Bake at 350 degrees for 10 to 12 minutes, until lightly golden. Remove cookies to wire racks; cool. Store in an airtight container. Makes about 4 dozen.

Christmas
Comfort Foods

Frosty Date & Walnut Snowballs

Chris Schank
Sandwich, IL

This melt-in-your-mouth cookie has been a family favorite for over 40 years! The recipe doubles easily. I like to cover these with lots of powdered sugar until the cookie trays are assembled.

1/2 c. butter, softened
1/3 c. powdered sugar, sifted
1 T. water
1 t. vanilla extract
1-1/4 c. all-purpose flour

1/8 t. salt
2/3 c. chopped dates
1/2 c. walnuts, finely chopped
Garnish: additional powdered
   sugar

In a large bowl, blend butter and powdered sugar; stir in water and vanilla. Add flour and salt; mix well. Stir in dates and walnuts. Roll dough into one-inch balls. Place on ungreased baking sheets, 2-1/2 inches apart. Bake at 300 degrees for about 20 minutes, until cookies are set but not brown. While still warm, roll in powdered sugar. Makes 2-1/2 dozen.

On Christmas Eve, don't forget to leave out cookies & milk for Santa. Treat the kids to cookies before bedtime too!

Sweet Treats to Share

Pecan-Carrot Bundt Cake

Judith Dudley
Hilton, NY

I've made this cake for family, special neighbors and the sheriff's department who patrol our town. Enjoy...it's moist and dee-lish!

1 c. chopped pecans, divided
15-1/4 oz. pkg. carrot cake mix
4 eggs, beaten
3/4 c. water

3/4 c. oil
16-oz. container coconut-pecan
   frosting

Spray a 9" or 10" Bundt® pan with non-stick vegetable spray. Sprinkle 1/2 cup pecans evenly in pan; set aside. In a large bowl, combine remaining pecans, dry cake mix, eggs, water and oil; beat well for 2 minutes. Stir in frosting. Pour batter into pan over pecans. Bake at 350 degrees for 50 to 60 minutes, until a toothpick inserted near the center comes out clean. Cook cake in pan for 5 to 10 minutes; turn out onto a cake plate. Allow to cool; slice to serve. Makes 8 to 12 servings.

Start a notebook of your favorite tried & true cookie recipes! Each Christmas, add notes about what worked well and what you'd do differently. Remember to label family members' favorites...even add snapshots of little bakers helping out. What a sweet tradition!

Christmas
Comfort Foods

Almond Squares

Margaret Welder
Madrid, IA

My daughter and I always get together before Christmas and bake many kinds of cookies. We like to give them out as gifts to people who have done something special for us during the year. This is one of our newer recipes...I put it together from several ideas. I make the cookies a bit smaller, since they go on a cookie plate.

8-oz. can almond paste
1 c. butter, softened
1/2 c. sugar
1/2 t. vanilla paste
3/4 t. almond extract, divided
2 c. all-purpose flour

2 egg yolks
4 t. water
2-oz. pkg. sliced almonds
13.4-oz. can dulce de leche
   caramel filling

Crumble almond paste into a large bowl. Beat with an electric mixer on medium speed until smooth, about one minute. Add butter and beat for about one minute. Add sugar, vanilla paste and 1/2 teaspoon extract; beat until smooth. Add flour; beat until combined. On a floured surface, roll out half of dough into a rectangle, 1/4-inch thick. Cut into 1-1/2 inch squares, using a ruler and a pizza cutter or a square cookie cutter. Place on parchment paper-lined baking sheets. In a small bowl, whisk together egg yolks, water and remaining extract; brush over half of cookies. Top these cookies with 2 sliced almonds each. Bake all cookies at 375 degrees for 7 to 9 minutes, until lightly golden. Remove to wire racks to cool. Add a scant teaspoon of caramel filling to each plain cookie; top with an almond-topped cookie. Makes 2 dozen.

Christmas waves a magic wand over this world,
and behold, everything is softer and more beautiful.

–Norman Vincent Peale

Sweet Treats
to Share

Coffee Toffee Bars

Nancy Kaiser
York, SC

I have been making these cookies for over 40 years. They're just a little different from the usual chocolate chip cookies and oh-so delicious.

1 c. butter
1 c. brown sugar, packed
1 egg, beaten
1 T. instant coffee granules
1 t. almond extract

2-1/4 c. all-purpose flour
1/2 t. baking powder
1/4 t. salt
1 c. semi-sweet chocolate chips
1/2 c. chopped walnuts

In a large bowl, blend together butter, brown sugar and egg. Stir in instant coffee and extract; set aside. In another bowl, mix together flour, baking powder and salt; add to butter mixture and mix well. Stir in chocolate chips and nuts. Press dough into a greased 15"x10" jelly-roll pan. Bake at 350 degrees for 20 to 25 minutes, until golden. Spread with Glaze while still warm; cut into bars. Makes 2 to 3 dozen.

Almond Glaze:

1 T. butter
3/4 c. powdered sugar

1/8 t. almond extract
1 to 2 T. milk

Combine all ingredients; mix together until smooth.

Need a sleighful of gifts for co-workers? Tuck in several wrapped Coffee Toffee Bars into vintage coffee mugs and wrap in festive cellophane...sure to be a hit!

Christmas
Comfort Foods

Cherry Delight

Robin Faison
Vero Beach, FL

This sweet dessert was always on Grandma's menu for holiday dinners. I still think of her when I fix it!

1-1/2 c. graham cracker crumbs
1 T. all-purpose flour
1/4 c. sugar
1/4 c. butter, melted
8-oz. pkg. cream cheese,
   softened

1 c. powdered sugar
16-oz. container frozen whipped
   topping, thawed
21-oz. can cherry pie filling

In a large bowl, mix together graham cracker crumbs, flour, sugar and melted butter. Press into the bottom and up the sides of an ungreased 13"x9" glass baking pan. Set in refrigerator to chill. In another bowl, blend together cream cheese, powdered sugar and whipped topping; spread over graham cracker crust. Top with pie filling. Cover and chill for several hours, until set; cut into squares. Makes 12 servings.

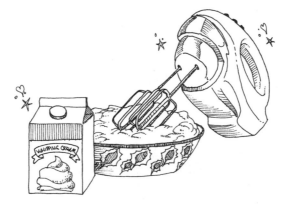

Nothing says "country-fresh flavor" like dollops of whipped cream on a warm homebaked dessert. In a chilled bowl, using chilled beaters, beat a cup of whipping cream on high speed until soft peaks form. Stir in 2 teaspoons sugar and 2 teaspoons vanilla extract...now, wasn't that easy?

Sweet Treats
to Share

Santa's Best Spritz Cookies

Paula Marchesi
Auburn, PA

I've been making these cookies since I was a little girl. I've tried every flavor extract I could find, and they were all delicious. These make nice gifts to give to friends, especially at Christmas

1 c. shortening
3/4 c. sugar
1 egg, beaten
1 t. almond extract
2-1/4 c. all-purpose flour

1/2 t. baking powder
Optional: 1/8 t. salt
Garnish: powdered sugar, colored
    sugar, candy sprinkles

In a large bowl, beat shortening and sugar until fluffy. Add egg and extract; mix well and set aside. In a separate bowl, combine flour, baking powder and salt, if using; add to shortening mixture and mix until blended. Spoon dough into a cookie press, fitted with decorative disc of your choice. Press cookies onto greased or parchment paper-lined baking sheets, 2 inches apart. Decorate with sugar or sprinkles as desired. Bake at 400 degrees for 7 to 8 minutes; do not allow to brown. Makes 6-1/2 dozen.

Make your own colored sugar. Place 1/2 cup sugar in a plastic zipping bag, then add 5 to 6 drops of food coloring. Knead the bag until color is mixed throughout, spread sugar on a baking sheet and let dry

Christmas Comfort Foods

Christmas Peppermint Cookies

Judy Borecky
Escondido, CA

*My own creation! I took a lemon drop cookie recipe, cut down the oil
and added some scrumptious icing to turn it into a peppermint cookie.
One cute idea for Christmas is to tint the dough green and make
Grinch cookies. After they have cooled, add a small dot of icing and
a red cinnamon candy heart. So sweet for the holidays!*

1/2 c. butter, softened	1/2 t. baking soda
1/4 c. oil	1/2 t. salt
1 egg, beaten	1/2 t. cream of tartar
1/2 c. powdered sugar	2 c. all-purpose flour
1/2 c. sugar	2 t. vanilla extract

Combine all ingredients in a large bowl; mix well. Cover and chill until
firm. Drop dough onto ungreased baking sheets, 3 level tablespoons
per cookie. Bake at 350 degrees for 10 to 12 minutes, until golden.
Remove cookies to wire racks; cool. Spread Icing over cookies.
Makes 1-1/2 dozen.

Icing:

1/4 c. butter, melted	1 drop red food coloring
1/8 t. salt	1/4 c. peppermint candies,
2 c. powdered sugar	crushed

Combine butter, salt and powdered sugar; mix well. Stir in food coloring;
fold in crushed candies.

To easily crush candy canes for holiday garnishes, place candy in a
plastic zipping bag and tap gently with a wooden mallet or rolling pin.

Sweet Treats
to Share

Easy Snowball Cookies

Linda Loput
Brea, CA

This was my sister Julie's favorite recipe for Snowball Cookies. Everyone waited for them every Christmas season, as she made hundreds of cookies every year to pass out to family, friends and her husband's co-workers. We do the same each year in her memory.

1 c. butter
1/2 c. powdered sugar
1 t. vanilla extract
2 c. all-purpose flour

1 c. chopped pecans
Garnish: additional powdered
    sugar

In a large bowl, mix butter until softened. Add powdered sugar; blend together. Stir in vanilla. Add flour; mix well. Stir in nuts. Roll into balls by teaspoonfuls; place on parchment paper-lined baking sheets. Bake at 350 degrees for 15 to 20 minutes, until bottoms are lightly golden. Cool slightly; roll in powdered sugar. Cool completely; roll again in more powdered sugar. Makes 2 dozen.

Emma's Shoebox Candy

Evangeline Boston
Bradley Junction, FL

Years ago, I worked with Emma at a hospital. At Christmas, she always brought this candy to work in a decorated shoebox. So, that's the origin of the name! It's very good, and easy to make.

12-oz. pkg. butterscotch chips
3 T. creamy peanut butter

3 c. corn flake cereal

In a large saucepan over low heat, melt butterscotch chips with peanut butter, stirring constantly. Add cereal; mix well. Drop by teaspoonfuls onto wax paper; let stand until set. Makes 2 dozen.

Save the plastic liners when you toss out empty cereal boxes. They're perfect for storing homebaked treats.

Christmas Comfort Foods

Swedish Almond Squares

Evelyn DeLutis
Bridgewater, MA

This cookie is a favorite in my Swedish family, but those who are not Swedish always ask for the recipe too. It's my favorite cookie with a cup of coffee. It is sooo easy, too. I usually double this recipe and bake in two pans, because it freezes well.

2 eggs
1 c. sugar
1 c. all-purpose flour
1/8 t. salt
2 t. almond extract

1/2 c. margarine, melted
1-1/4 c. slivered almonds
Garnish: additional sugar or
    Swedish pearl sugar

In a large bowl, beat eggs thoroughly by hand. Gradually stir in sugar; set aside. In another bowl, sift together flour and salt; gradually add to egg mixture and mix well. Add extract and melted margarine; mix well. Spread batter in a 10"x8" disposable aluminum baking pan coated with non-stick vegetable spray. Sprinkle with almonds and additional sugar or Swedish pearl sugar. Bake at 325 degrees for 25 minutes, or until edges are just beginning to turn golden. Do not overbake, or cookies will be too dry. Cool; cut into squares. Makes 16 cookies.

...le everyone in the car and head to the local cut-your-own tree farm. ...re's almost always hot cocoa and cookies to share, and sometimes, even a surprise visit from Santa & Mrs. Claus!

Sweet Treats
to Share

Mowe's Pound Cake

Kayla Herring
Hartwell, GA

My Grandmother Bertie made this recipe for every Thanksgiving, Christmas and Easter. It is my mom's favorite cake, and she chose it for her birthday every year. My grandmother is no longer here, but we cherish her recipe and think of her often whenever we have a pound cake. The name of the recipe is Mowe's Pound Cake, because that's what I called her as a child.

2 c. butter or shortening
2-2/3 c. sugar
8 eggs
3-1/2 c. all-purpose flour

1/2 c. whipping cream
1 t. vanilla extract
1/2 t. lemon extract
1/2 t. almond extract

In a large bowl, stir butter or shortening until softened. Stir in sugar, a little at a time. Add eggs, one at a time, mixing well after each. Add flour, cream and extracts; mix well. Pour batter into a tube pan greased with shortening. Bake at 350 degrees for one hour and 40 minutes. Cool; turn out of pan and slice to serve. Makes 16 servings.

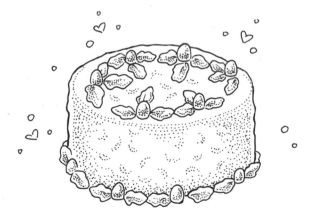

Dress up a frosted cake with beautiful red and green "leaves." Lightly dust a work surface with sugar and roll red and green gumdrops until flat. Use a leaf-shaped mini cookie cutter to make leaves. Sweet and simple!

Christmas
Comfort Foods

Fabulous Lemon & Orange Sugar Cookies

Judy Smith
Bellevue, WA

I received this recipe from my mother in the 1960s. Mother always made the cookies during the holiday season each year, which the family enjoyed. They're still a favorite.

1/2 c. butter, softened
1/2 t. salt
1 t. lemon zest
1 c. sugar
2 eggs, beaten
2 t. orange zest
2 c. all-purpose flour

1 t. baking powder
1/2 t. baking soda
2 T. orange juice
2/3 c. flaked coconut
Garnish: additional 1/4 c. sugar,
    1/2 t. orange zest

Combine all ingredients except garnish in a large bowl; mix well. Drop dough by teaspoonfuls onto greased baking sheets. Flatten cookies by stamping with a flat-bottomed glass tumbler, covered with a damp cloth. Combine additional sugar and orange zest; sprinkle over cookies. Bake at 350 degrees for 10 to 12 minutes. Makes about 2-1/2 dozen.

Send a Christmas cookie party in a box! When wrapping up gift boxes of homebaked cookies, why not tuck in a packet of paper holiday napkins and a box of spiced tea?

Sweet Treats
to Share

Almond Shortbread

Jessica Kraus
Delaware, OH

This is such a wonderful recipe. It's so simple that even if you aren't a baker, you will master it! Enjoy with a cup of hot coffee or tea.

3/4 c. butter, melted
1-1/2 c. plus 1 T. sugar, divided
2 eggs
1-1/2 c. all-purpose flour

1/2 t. salt
1 t. almond extract
1/2 c. sliced almonds

Line a 10" cast-iron skillet or round cake pan with aluminum foil, allowing foil to hang over the sides of the pan. Spray foil with non-stick vegetable spray; set aside. Add melted butter to a large bowl; stir in 1-1/2 cups sugar. Beat in eggs, one at a time. Add flour and salt; mix well. Add extract; stir well. Pour batter into skillet, spreading to cover the entire bottom. Top with almonds and remaining sugar. Bake at 350 degrees for about 35 minutes, until lightly golden on top. Remove from oven. Cool completely; use foil to lift shortbread from skillet. Remove foil; place on a cutting board and cut into wedges. Makes 8 servings.

Host a holiday tea party for your friends. It's so nice
to relax and catch up with one another!

Christmas
Comfort Foods

Pecan Sugar Cookies

Joyce Roebuck
Jacksonville, TX

These cookies are really good! I've made them so many times and always take the recipe along, as someone always asks for it.

2 c. all-purpose flour
1/2 t. baking soda
1/2 t. cream of tartar
1/2 t. salt
1/2 c. butter, softened
1/2 c. oil

1/2 c. sugar
1/2 c. powdered sugar
1 egg, beaten
1/2 t. vanilla extract
1 c. chopped pecans

In a bowl, mix together flour, baking soda, cream of tartar and salt; set aside. In another bowl, beat together butter, oil, sugars, egg and vanilla. Gradually beat flour mixture into butter mixture; stir in pecans. Form dough into balls by heaping teaspoonfuls; place on ungreased baking sheets. Press down balls with a fork. Bake at 350 degrees for 10 to 12 minutes, until golden. Makes about 3 dozen.

Fruit & Chips Cookies

Penny Sherman
Ava, MO

There's something for everybody in these yummy cookies.

1 c. butter, softened
3/4 c. brown sugar, packed
1/2 c. sugar
1 t. baking soda
2 eggs, beaten

1 t. vanilla extract
2 c. all-purpose flour
2 c. granola cereal
1-1/2 c. mixed dried fruit, diced
1 c. white chocolate chips

In a large bowl, combine butter, sugars and baking soda; blend well. Add eggs and vanilla; stir well. Gradually stir in flour until well mixed. Fold in remaining ingredients. Drop dough onto ungreased baking sheets by rounded teaspoonfuls, 2 inches apart. Flatten slightly. Bake at 350 degrees for about 10 minutes, until edges are golden. Cool for one minute; remove cookies to wire racks and cool completely. Makes 5 dozen.

Sweet Treats to Share

Marvelous Butterscotch Squares
Lisa Hains
Ontario, Canada

These ten-minute marvels will melt in your mouth...but try to let them harden first to share with others, if you can!

11-oz. pkg. butterscotch chips
1/2 c. crunchy peanut butter
1/4 c. butter
1 to 2 T. oil
1-1/4 c. crispy rice cereal
3 c. mini marshmallows

In a saucepan, combine butterscotch chips, peanut butter, butter and one tablespoon oil. Cook over medium-low heat, stirring often, until completely melted and the consistency of cake batter. If mixture begins to thicken or "seize," stir in remaining oil. While mixture is still hot and soft, stir in cereal. Let stand about 4 minutes, until cooled slightly. Fold in marshmallows; let stand until marshmallows are melted. Stir to blend. Spread mixture in a greased 8"x8" baking pan. Cool; cut into squares. Cover and refrigerate until set. Makes 16 squares.

On baking day, pop up a big bowl of fresh popcorn.
The kids (and you!) will have something tasty to nibble on,
saving the nuts and chocolate chips for the cookies.

Christmas
Comfort Foods

Old-Timey Chocolate Fudge

Anita Polizzi
Bakersville, NC

This recipe is from an old Home Comfort wood cookstove cookbook. My grandparents bought the stove in the 1930s and this cookbook came with the stove. My grandmother used the cookbook all the time...the pages are stained and well used. I think it's the only cookbook she ever had, and I treasure it today. We made this candy often, and my grandfather loved it. My fondest memory is of eating the tiny bit of candy off her finger after she dropped it in a cup of water for the soft-ball stage.

2 c. sugar
1 T. baking cocoa
1/2 c. milk

2 T. butter, sliced
1 t. vanilla extract
Optional: 1 c. chopped nuts

Combine sugar, cocoa and milk in a deep cast-iron skillet or heavy saucepan. Cook and stir over low heat until sugar is dissolved. Continue cooking over low heat until mixture reaches the soft-ball stage, or 234 to 243 degrees on a candy thermometer. Do not stir the hot mixture unless it threatens to burn after reaching the boiling point. Remove from stove and add butter; do not stir. Allow to cool. If you are in a hurry, set the pan in a sink filled with cold water. Add vanilla; beat mixture with a spoon until it is creamy and beginning to thicken. Just before it is ready to pour out on a platter, stir in nuts, if using. Pour into a greased platter. Cut into squares before fudge hardens. Makes 2 to 3 dozen.

Buttering the sides of a heavy saucepan before adding fudge ingredients will help prevent sugar crystals from forming on the pan. This will keep fudge creamy, smooth and delicious!

Sweet Treats to Share

Santa's Whiskers

Jennifer Hatridge
Springfield, ME

This unique cookie recipe has no eggs and the yummy coconut edges will remind you of Santa's whiskers! They are a favorite holiday cookie in my family. I have found that the easiest way to chop the sticky candied cherries is with the blade attachment on my mini food processor.

1 c. butter, softened
1 c. sugar
2 T. milk
1 t. vanilla extract
2-1/2 c. all-purpose flour

3/4 c. candied red cherries,
    finely chopped
1/2 c. pecans, finely chopped
3/4 c. flaked coconut

In a bowl, blend together butter and sugar; blend in milk and vanilla. Stir in flour; fold in cherries and pecans. Dough will be stiff. Form dough into 2 rolls, each 8 inches long. Roll in coconut to coat outside of rolls; wrap separately in wax paper. Refrigerate at least one hour and up to one week. When ready to bake, slice each roll into 1/4-inch slices. Place on ungreased baking sheets. Bake at 375 degrees for 10 to 12 minutes, until edges are golden. Makes 4 to 5 dozen.

Host a cookie swap...a terrific way to get a variety of yummy cookies! Invite 6 to 8 friends and ask them to bring a half dozen cookies for each guest, plus copies of the recipe. Everyone takes as many home...yum!

Christmas
Comfort Foods

Elisa's No–Bake Fruitcake

*Shirley Howie
Foxboro, MA*

This easy recipe was given to me many years ago by a very dear friend. I usually make it a few weeks before Christmas, to allow all the wonderful flavors to blend. I like to serve slices of fruitcake alongside my Christmas cookies for variety.

13-1/2 oz. pkg. graham
   cracker crumbs
2 t. orange zest
1 t. lemon zest
1 t. cinnamon
1/4 t. ground cloves
1/4 t. ground ginger
1/4 t. allspice

8-oz. pkg. chopped dates
8-oz. pkg. mixed candied fruit
1 c. golden raisins
1 c. chopped walnuts
1/2 c. honey
1/2 c. orange juice
2 T. lemon juice

In a large bowl, combine graham cracker crumbs, citrus zests and spices; blend thoroughly. Add dates, fruit, raisins and walnuts; mix well and set aside. In a separate bowl, beat together honey and citrus juices; add to crumb mixture and blend thoroughly. Pack mixture firmly into a greased 8"x4" disposable aluminum loaf pan. Cover and refrigerate for at least 2 days. Let stand about 2 hours at room temperature before serving. Slice and serve. Makes 16 servings.

Use kitchen shears to make short work of cutting up gumdrops, candied fruit, dates and other sticky cookie ingredients.

Sweet Treats
to Share

Megan's Cowgirl Cookies

Wendy Jo Minotte
Duluth, MN

These cookies don't last long...everyone loves them! My daughter Megan makes them for our family every year at Christmastime. She always gives her dad his very own batch that he's not required to share with anyone, as they are his favorite.

1 egg, lightly beaten
1/2 c. butter
1 t. vanilla extract
1-1/3 c. all-purpose flour
1 t. baking powder
1 t. baking soda

1/4 t. salt
1/2 c. brown sugar, packed
1/2 c. sugar
1 c. long-cooking oats, uncooked
3/4 c. candy-coated chocolates
3/4 c. white chocolate chips

In a bowl, blend egg, butter and vanilla; set aside. In a large bowl, mix together remaining ingredients. Add egg mixture; use the back of a large spoon (or your hands) to mix everything together. Roll dough into 1-1/2 inch balls. Arrange on ungreased baking sheets, 4 rows on each sheet. Bake at 350 degrees for 10 to 12 minutes. Cookies will be soft when removed from the oven; allow them to cool on the baking sheets and they will firm up. Makes 2 dozen.

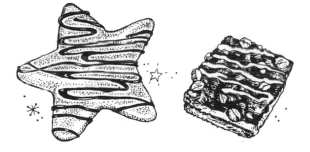

Dress up any kind of cookie with a drizzle of melted white or semi-sweet chocolate chips. Simply place chips in a small zipping bag and microwave briefly, until melted. Snip off a tiny corner and squeeze to drizzle. Afterwards, just toss away the bag...couldn't be easier!

Christmas
Comfort Foods

Apricot Thimble-Its

Carol Gray
Sammamish, WA

When my son was little, he loved these cookies that my mom made when he visited her. He called them "cookie pies" because they looked like little pies. My son is now in his 40s and still calls them Grandma's cookie pies. If you're short on time, apricot jam can be used instead of the cooked filling.

1 c. brown sugar, packed	2-1/4 c. all-purpose flour
2/3 c. shortening	1 t. baking powder
1 egg, beaten	1/2 t. baking soda
1 t. orange zest	3 T. milk
1 t. salt	

Make Apricot Filling; set aside to cool. In a bowl, combine brown sugar, shortening, egg, orange zest and salt; beat thoroughly. Add flour, baking powder and baking soda; blend well. Stir in milk. Cover and chill dough for one hour. On a floured surface, roll out dough 1/8-inch thick; cut dough with a 2-1/2 inch round cookie cutter. Place half of cookies on greased baking sheets; top each with one teaspoonful apricot filling. With a thimble, cut out centers of remaining cookies, or cut a slit with a knife. Place on filled cookies; press edges with fork to seal. Bake at 375 degrees for 8 to 10 minutes. Makes 2 to 2-1/2 dozen.

Apricot Filling:

6-oz. pkg. dried apricots	1 T. orange juice
1-1/2 c. water	1/2 c. sugar

Combine apricots and water in a small saucepan; bring to boil. Reduce heat to medium-low; cook for 15 minutes. Drain; reserve 6 tablespoons juice. Mash apricots to a smooth pulp; return to pan. Add reserved apricot juice, orange juice and sugar. Cook over low heat until thickened; cool.

Fill a tall apothecary jar with old-fashioned rock candy sticks in bright colors to use as hot beverage stirrers.

Sweet Treats
to Share

Almond Butter Crunch

JoAnn
Gooseberry Patch

This homemade candy is simple to make and really scrumptious.

1/2 c. plus 1 T. butter, divided
1 c. slivered almonds

1/2 c. sugar
1 T. light corn syrup

Line a 9" round cake pan with aluminum foil; coat well with one tablespoon butter and set aside. In a heavy 10" skillet over medium heat, combine remaining butter, almonds, sugar and corn syrup. Cook, stirring constantly, for about 10 minutes, until sugar is melted and mixture turns golden. Quickly spread mixture into pan. Cool for 15 minutes, or until firm. Remove candy by lifting edges of foil. Peel off foil; break candy into pieces. Store in a lightly covered container. Makes about 20 pieces.

Peanut Butter Balls

Joie Cunningham
Wrightstown, WI

I make batches and batches of these at Christmas!

1/4 c. butter, softened
2 c. graham crackers, crushed
2 c. powdered sugar

2 c. creamy peanut butter
1 lb. dipping chocolate

Combine all ingredients except chocolate in a large bowl; mix well. Cover and chill at least one hour. Roll into one-inch balls; place on parchment paper-lined baking sheets. Chill. Melt chocolate in a double boiler; dip balls into chocolate. Return to baking sheets and chill until set. Store in refrigerator. Makes 5 to 6 dozen.

Place Peanut Butter Balls in paper muffin liners and set on a platter... oh-so easy for everyone to serve themselves at a dessert party.

Christmas
Comfort Foods

Pumpkin-Pecan Cake

Denise Evans
Moosic, PA

This cake is really delicious, yet so easy to make. I love it when nuts cover the whole top of the cake! If you don't want to spring for pecans, you can use walnuts. Both are good...pecans are best!

1 c. sugar
1-1/4 t. pumpkin pie spice
29-oz. can pumpkin pie filling
2 eggs, beaten
12-oz. can evaporated milk

18-1/2 oz. pkg. white cake mix
16-oz. pkg. chopped pecans
   or walnuts
1 c. butter, melted
Optional: vanilla ice cream

In a large bowl, combine sugar, spice, pumpkin pie filling, eggs and evaporated milk; stir well. Pour batter into an ungreased 13"x9" baking pan. Sprinkle with dry cake mix and chopped nuts; drizzle with melted butter. Bake at 350 degrees for one hour and 15 minutes. Cool completely. Cut into squares to serve, topped with a scoop of ice cream, if desired. Makes 15 servings.

Wrap up Grandmother's big yellowware mixing bowl
along with her prized cookie recipe for a daughter who's
learning to bake. She'll love it!

Sweet Treats
to Share

Holiday Poke Cake

Debi Hodges
Frederica, DE

A festive dessert to serve during the holidays. My family absolutely loves it! I like to make my own Buttercream Frosting, but canned vanilla frosting is just fine too.

18-1/2 oz. pkg. white cake mix
3-oz. pkg. cherry or strawberry
　gelatin mix
3-oz. pkg. lime gelatin mix

2 c. boiling water, divided
Optional: colored sugar or
　candy sprinkles

Prepare and bake cake as package directs, using a well-greased 13"x9" baking pan. Remove from oven; poke cake with a large fork at 1/2-inch intervals and set aside. Add gelatin mixes to 2 bowls. Pour one cup boiling water into each mix and stir until dissolved. Pour gelatins separately over baked cake, alternating rows of color. Refrigerate cake for at least 3 hours. Dip bottom of cake pan into warm water for 10 seconds; turn out cake onto a serving platter. Spread with Buttercream Frosting; decorate as desired. Keep chilled until serving time; cut into squares. Serves 12.

Buttercream Frosting:

1/2 c. shortening
1/2 c. butter, softened
1 t. vanilla extract

4 c. powdered sugar, divided
2 T. milk

Beat shortening and butter with an electric mixer on medium speed until light and fluffy. Beat in vanilla. On low speed, gradually beat in powdered sugar, one cup at a time; beat well on medium speed. Frosting will appear dry and stiff. Beat in small amounts of milk to desired consistency; continue to beat on medium speed until light and fluffy.

For a perfectly smooth finish when you're frosting a cake with buttercream frosting, dip a metal spatula in very hot water, wipe it dry and gently glide the spatula over the frosting.

Christmas
Comfort Foods

Santa's Most-Requested Cookies

Stephanie Turner
Meridian, ID

My daughters and I have been making these cookies for Santa on Christmas Eve for years. Santa is such a fan that every year, about a week before Christmas, we get a letter from him personally requesting we make the cookies again! I think he's a big fan of mint and chocolate. Use candies in seasonal colors, if you can.

2-1/4 c. all-purpose flour
1 t. baking soda
1/2 t. salt
1 c. butter, softened
1 c. brown sugar, packed
1/2 c. sugar

2 eggs
2 t. vanilla extract
11-1/2 oz. pkg. milk chocolate
chips
1 c. candy-coated mint-flavored
chocolates

In a bowl, whisk together flour, baking soda and salt; set aside. In a large bowl, with an electric mixer on medium speed, beat butter with sugars until creamy and lightened in color. Add eggs and vanilla, one at a time; beat on low speed until well mixed. Gradually stir flour mixture into butter mixture. Stir in chocolate chips and candies. Using a cookie scoop, drop dough by tablespoonfuls onto parchment paper-lined baking sheets, about 2 inches apart. For soft, chewy cookies, bake at 350 degrees for 9 to 11 minutes, until just beginning to turn golden around the edges, or one to 2 minutes longer for crisper cookies. Makes 4 dozen.

To keep cookies extra soft, store in an airtight container with a slice of white bread, changing the bread everyday.

Sweet Treats
to Share

Beulah's English Toffee Bars

Pat Beach
Fisherville, KY

This delicious recipe was shared with me years ago by a sweet elderly volunteer at the medical office where I worked. She loved baking and brought in goodies such as this to share with the staff every Friday. We all laughed and said she was trying her best to make us gain weight!

1 c. butter, softened
1 c. brown sugar, packed
1 egg yolk
1 t. vanilla extract

2 c. all-purpose flour
6-oz. pkg. semi-sweet chocolate chips
3/4 c. chopped pecans

In a large bowl, blend butter and brown sugar. Add egg yolk, vanilla and flour; mix well. Spread dough in an ungreased 13"x9" baking pan. Bake at 350 degrees for about 30 to 35 minutes, until lightly golden. Remove from oven; sprinkle evenly with chocolate chips. Return to oven for 2 to 3 minutes, until chocolate chips melt. Spread melted chocolate evenly over the top. Sprinkle pecans evenly over chocolate. Cut into squares while still warm and serve. Makes one dozen.

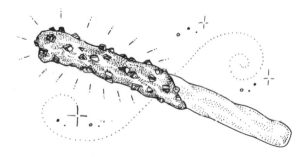

Turn mini pretzel twists into scrumptious candy box treats.
Simply dip in melted chocolate and decorate with a toss
of colorful sprinkles.

Christmas
Comfort Foods

Horseshoes

This is my husband's favorite cookie recipe that his mother used to make at Christmas. They're very easy to make, and both the dough and the cookies freeze well. Everyone who tries them, loves them... great with hot coffee!

1 lb. butter, softened
1-1/4 c. buttermilk
4 t. vanilla extract

2 egg yolks
4 c. all-purpose flour
Garnish: powdered sugar

In a large bowl, combine all ingredients except garnish; mix well. Dough will be sticky. Separate dough into 3 portions; wrap each in plastic wrap and refrigerate at least 6 hours or overnight. (At this point, dough can also be frozen.) On a floured surface, roll out one portion of dough into a 10-inch circle, 1/8-inch thick; set aside. Sprinkle 1/3 of Walnut Filling generously onto dough; cut into triangle slices. Roll up each triangle from the wider end, shaping crescent-roll style. Place on a parchment paper-lined baking sheet. Repeat with remaining dough and filling. Bake at 375 degrees for 10 to 12 minutes, until golden. Cool; sprinkle with powdered sugar. To freeze, cool cookies but do not add powdered sugar; place in a freezer container and freeze. At serving time, thaw and sprinkle with powdered sugar. Makes 3 dozen.

Walnut Filling:

3/4 c. brown sugar, packed
1 c. sugar

2 t. cinnamon
1 c. walnuts, finely chopped

Combine all ingredients; mix well.

Christmas! The very word brings joy to our hearts.
–Joan Winmill Brown

Sweet Treats
to Share

Reindeer Droppings

Linda Roper
Pine Mountain, GA

My children, grandchildren and friends love this tasty treat! I make it every Christmas for family & friends and pack in candy tins. I am asked for this recipe all the time. So rich and delicious...it will disappear quickly!

16-oz. jar honey-roasted peanuts
2 16-oz. pkgs. white chocolate
  chips
12-oz. pkg. milk chocolate chips
4-oz. pkg. German chocolate
  baking chocolate, broken

12-oz. pkg. butterscotch chips
2 12-oz. pkgs. candy-coated
  chocolates
12-oz. pkg. brickle toffee
  baking bits

In a greased 6-quart slow cooker, combine peanuts, white and milk chocolate chips and baking chocolate. Cover and cook on low setting for 2 hours, or until chocolate is melted. Stir well. Add remaining ingredients; mix well. Drop mixture by tablespoonfuls onto parchment paper-lined baking sheets; allow to set. Store in an airtight container. Makes 6 to 7 dozen.

Whip up some cute treat bags for Reindeer Droppings in a jiffy! To mini gift totes, glue 2 google eyes and a big red pompom nose. Tuck in treats, then glue a candy cane at each side of the bag. Sweet!

Christmas Comfort Foods

Jumble Jubilies

Vicki Karras
Dickinson, ND

My children are now grown up, and they still ask for these cake-like cookies at Christmastime. Be sure to frost them while still warm! For a variation, instead of chopped walnuts, use one cup shredded coconut, dates, raisins or semi-sweet chocolate chips.

1/2 c. margarine, softened	1 t. vanilla extract
1 c. brown sugar, packed	2-3/4 to 3 c. all-purpose flour
1/2 c. sugar	1/2 t. baking soda
2 eggs	1 t. salt
1 c. evaporated milk	1 c. chopped walnuts

In a large bowl, mix margarine, sugars and eggs thoroughly. Stir in evaporated milk and vanilla; set aside. In another bowl, mix together flour, baking soda and salt; add to margarine mixture and mix well. Fold in nuts. Cover and chill for about one to 2 hours. Drop dough by rounded tablespoonfuls onto greased baking sheets, 2 inches apart. Bake at 375 degrees for 10 minutes, or until golden. While cookies are still warm, frost with Burnt Butter Frosting. Makes 4 dozen.

Burnt Butter Frosting:

2 T. butter	1/4 c. evaporated milk
2 to 3 c. powdered sugar	Optional: few drops food coloring

Melt butter in a saucepan over medium heat; cook until dark golden. Stir in powdered sugar and evaporated milk until smooth. Add food coloring, if desired.

A sweet centerpiece...place a plump pillar candle on a clear glass dish and surround it with peppermint candies.

Sweet Treats
to Share

Coffee Ice Cream Punch

Joyce Roebuck
Jacksonville, TX

*This is wonderful! I've made this punch many times for
parties and showers. It's always a hit. Enjoy!*

1 c. water
2-oz. jar instant coffee granules
2 c. sugar

1 gal. whole milk
1/2 gal. chocolate ice cream
1/2 gal. vanilla ice cream

In a saucepan over high heat, bring water to a boil. Stir in coffee
granules and sugar; cook and stir until dissolved. Cover and chill for
30 minutes to overnight. At serving time, pour coffee mixture into a
punch bowl. Add milk and ice creams; mix gently until most of ice
cream is melted. Makes 20 servings.

Holiday Cranberry Tea

Marcy Gober
Murfreesboro, TN

*A delicious and festive tea for all holiday gatherings. Our family
likes to serve it when guests arrive or alongside desserts.*

4 qts. water
4 family-size tea bags
12-oz. can frozen lemonade
  concentrate, thawed
12-oz. can frozen orange juice
  concentrate, thawed

12-oz. can frozen pineapple juice
  concentrate, thawed
8-oz. can cranberry-raspberry
  juice cocktail

Bring water to a boil in a stockpot; add tea bags. Let stand for 3 to
5 minutes; discard tea bags and set aside. In a 6-quart slow cooker,
combine all juice concentrates; add 9 juice cans water. Add tea and
cranberry juice; stir. Cover and cook on low setting for 2 hours, or until
hot. Makes 25 servings.

Gather up those mismatched tea cups, set a tea light inside and
line them up along the mantel for a beautiful holiday glow.
So warm and inviting when friends are visiting.

Christmas
Comfort Foods

Merry Christmas Bars

Jennie Gist
Gooseberry Patch

These scrumptious bar cookies are chock-full of goodies like chocolate chips, fruit and nuts...sure to be a big hit! For cookie plates, dress them up with a drizzle of melted chocolate.

3/4 c. semi-sweet chocolate chips
3/4 c. raisins
1/2 c. maraschino cherry halves,
   well drained
1/2 c. chopped walnuts
1 c. plus 2 T. all-purpose flour,
   divided

1/3 c. butter, softened
1-1/2 c. brown sugar, packed
2 eggs, beaten
1 t. baking powder
1/2 t. salt
1 t. vanilla extract

In a large bowl, combine chocolate chips, raisins, cherries, walnuts and 2 tablespoons flour; set aside. In another bowl, beat butter, brown sugar and eggs until fluffy. Blend in remaining flour, baking powder, salt and vanilla; mix well. Stir in chocolate chip mixture. Spread batter evenly in a greased 11"x7" baking pan. Bake at 350 degrees for about 40 minutes, until a toothpick inserted in center comes out clean. Cool in pan; cut into bars. Makes about 2 dozen.

Make frosted bar cookies look extra-special! Lightly press
a cookie cutter into the frosting, then use a tube of
contrast-color frosting to trace the outline.

Sweet Treats to Share

Peppermint Dazzler

Katie Majeske
Denver, PA

My childhood took place in the 60s, and for as far back as I can remember, this was our special dessert at every Christmas. It's delicious, and looks so festive with the crushed candy canes on top.

2 c. graham cracker crumbs
1/2 c. butter, melted
1 1/2 c. powdered sugar
1/2 c. butter, softened
3 pasteurized eggs, beaten
2 sqs. bittersweet baking
   chocolate, melted

8-oz. container frozen whipped
   topping, thawed
1/2 of a 16-oz. pkg. mini
   marshmallows
1/2 c. peppermint candy canes,
   crushed

In a bowl, blend together graham cracker crumbs and melted butter. Press into the bottom of a greased 13"x9" baking pan; set aside. In another bowl, blend together powdered sugar and softened butter. Add eggs and chocolate; beat until light and fluffy. Spoon over crumb crust. Spoon whipped topping into a separate bowl; gently fold in marshmallows and spoon over chocolate layer. Sprinkle with crushed candy. Cover; keep refrigerated. Cut into squares. Serves 12 to 16.

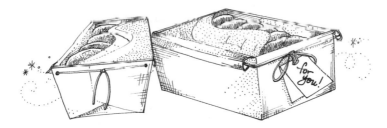

Mailing cookies to a friend? Select sturdy cookies that won't crumble easily. Bar cookies, brownies and drop cookies travel well, while frosted or filled cookies may be too soft.

INDEX

INDEX

INDEX

Find Gooseberry Patch
wherever you are!

www.gooseberrypatch.com

Call us toll-free at 1·800·854·6673

U.S. to Metric Recipe Equivalents

Volume Measurements

1/4 teaspoon	1 mL
1/2 teaspoon	2 mL
1 teaspoon	5 mL
1 tablespoon = 3 teaspoons	15 mL
2 tablespoons = 1 fluid ounce	30 mL
1/4 cup	60 mL
1/3 cup	75 mL
1/2 cup = 4 fluid ounces	125 mL
1 cup = 8 fluid ounces	250 mL
2 cups = 1 pint =16 fluid ounces	500 mL
4 cups = 1 quart	1 L

Weights

1 ounce	30 g
4 ounces	120 g
8 ounces	225 g
16 ounces = 1 pound	450 g

Oven Temperatures

300° F	150° C
325° F	160° C
350° F	180° C
375° F	190° C
400° F	200° C
450° F	230° C

Baking Pan Sizes

Square		Loaf	
8x8x2 inches	2 L = 20x20x5 cm	9x5x3 inches	2 L = 23x13x7 cm
9x9x2 inches	2.5 L = 23x23x5 cm	Round	
Rectangular		8x1-1/2 inches	1.2 L = 20x4 cm
13x9x2 inches	3.5 L = 33x23x5 cm	9x1-1/2 inches	1.5 L = 23x4 cm